Linkedin
Riche$

DEDICATION

For Sara, who has always believed in me.
I love you, my princess!

Linkedin Riche$

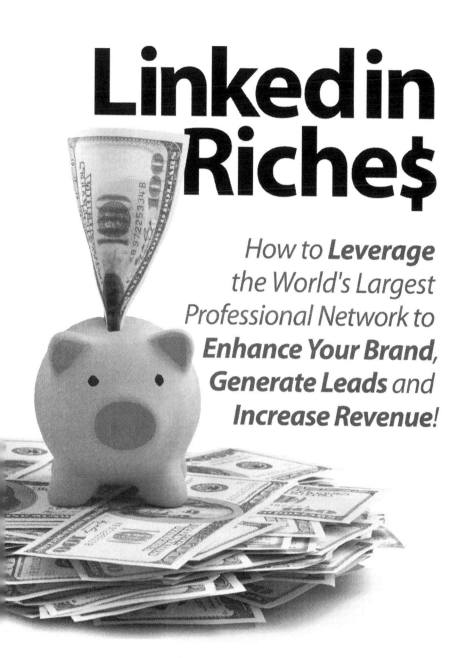

How to **Leverage** the World's Largest Professional Network to **Enhance Your Brand, Generate Leads** and **Increase Revenue!**

John **Nemo**

LinkedIn Riches

Book cover and interior design by Gregory Rohm

Printed in the United States of America

TESTIMONIALS

I cannot recommend highly enough the benefits of this book. Following John Nemo's strategies has unleashed a whole new world of how to *really* use LinkedIn for my business. If you haven't read John's book or attended one of his live trainings or webinars, stop what you are doing, sign up and have your eyes opened, the man is a genius!"

 – JAMES COOKE, *Commercial Debt Management Consultant, Debt Collection Master Agent*

"John is a masterful visionary that has seen the true value of LinkedIn if used properly. His teaching methods are exceptional. Utilizing his self-paced style and his creative approach to the material is refreshing. If you're serious about learning new and innovative techniques, John is your man!"

 – RICH LUCIA, Speaker & Author of *The 180 Rule*

"I went through one of John's free webinars on LinkedIn Riches. I got more out of that free hour than I have most full paid days of training! Since then I have viewed John's other material, and found it insightful, eye opening, revelation inspiring, and filled with clear cut, easy-to-execute action items that pay dividends immediately. I don't think any of you should use LinkedIn to market yourself or your company, or even read this book. That's less competition for me!"

 – ROGER WEISS, IFCCE, *Professional Speaker & Trainer, Debt Collections & Training Consultant*

TESTIMONIALS

"I have been working with LinkedIn for a few years now and have sat through several presentations on how to 'Maximize Your Profile,' 'How to Attract Others' and similar subjects. I have never sat through a LinkedIn presentation that had as much value as John Nemo's did in such a short time. I took away three things that I will be implementing *immediately* and know that they will have a positive effect on our bottom line in the next 90 days. John is truly an expert in his field … people would be *silly* not to make the time and invest the money in this amazing book!"

— GINGER ZEMLA, *Managing Member, Innovative Principle Strategies*

"John is one of the most knowledgeable LinkedIn experts. Period. I took his course and through an hour consultation he walked me through the key aspects of this platform that would get me results immediately. I recommend that anyone who wants to learn how to use LinkedIn for business, learn from John he'll get you results!"

— BILLYE THOMPSON, *Owner, Cayenne Marketing Consultants*

TESTIMONIALS

"After implementing what I learned from John about LinkedIn, I became top 4 out of 1 million searches for my profile, and that is just the beginning! I strongly recommend listening to what John has to say and implementing the changes to the way you market yourself to your clients and prospects. I look forward to working more with John in the future!"

– JARED MEAYS, *Sales Executive, The Harry A. Koch Co.*

"John is a very innovative and inspirational person and his service and personality are very unique. His LinkedIn training is a MUST for any business who wants to expand their client base, and utilize the full potential of LinkedIn. I was amazed at how insightful John's teaching was. I have found John and his program to be a valuable asset for my company and me. Keep up the good work John!"

– RICK JOHNSON, *Lions & Associates, LLC*

ALSO BY **JOHN NEMO**

FICTION

Miller's Miracle   Jumper   The King's Game

NONFICTION

(Mostly) True Stories:
47 Essays on the Laughter of Life

Share This:
Labor Unions and Social Media

Table *of* Contents

10   **Author's Note**

12   **Introduction: Why LinkedIn?**

18   **Chapter 1 - Profiles:** Why 99 percent of people are *still* using LinkedIn the wrong way!

42   **Chapter 2 – Prospects:** How to instantly locate your ideal customers on LinkedIn no matter what industry you're in!

48   **Chapter 3 – Personality:** How to engage your ideal prospects on LinkedIn by creating instant likability and trust!

64   **Chapter 4 – Profits:** How to turn LinkedIn Groups into your own personal ATM Machine!

86   **Chapter 5 – Proven:** How to create content on LinkedIn that establishes your credibility and attracts your ideal customers!

100   **Chapter 6 – Prophesy:** Where is LinkedIn headed?

104   **Bonuses + Resources**

110   **More About the Author**

AUTHOR'S NOTE

There are many to thank, but none are more important to me than Jesus Christ. Your undeserved love, your jaw-dropping grace, your incredible sacrifice ... how am I supposed to put into words all that you are? Jesus, I can't wait until the day I step into heaven. I'm going to burst through the doors, running, and leap into your waiting arms. I'm going to wrap my arms around your neck, and I'm going to hold onto you, and sob tears of joy, and I'm going to say, "Never let go of me, *ever!*" And you are going to smile, and say gently over my sobs and shaking, "I never did, John. I never did."

Jesus is a tough act to follow, but I've got to thank some other folks too. I'll start with John Morgan, who has been an indispensible part of my life and business for the past 18 months. Reading his book *Brand Against The Machine* changed the entire way I approach marketing and business, and his advice and inspiration remain incredibly important to me. Thank you, John!

Thanks to my good friend Gregory Rohm, who designed the book you now hold in your hands. He's the most talented graphic designer I've ever met, and I'm thankful to have had him in my corner for this and so many other projects.

I want to thank my parents (both English teachers!) for fostering a love of story and books early in my life. I literally grew up in a house that had floor-to-ceiling bookshelves lining the walls of our family room.

To all the great business authors I've read and learned so much from – Dale Carnegie, Nancy Duarte, Keith Ferrazi, Chip and Dan Heath, Erik Qualman and Dan Pink – thank you for inspiring and teaching me about so many important topics related to business, networking, storytelling, presentations, social media, selling and more!

To the irrepressible Gary Vaynerchuk, who has been inspiring me and countless other entrepreneurs and business owners for almost a decade – thank you!

To all the great teachers I've had – Dave Nimmer, Chris Kachian, Bud Paape, Pat Maroney, Sister Marylin – your impact is life-long in its breadth and scope. What an amazing calling you've chosen!

To my gorgeous wife, Sara, and our three wild boys – Jacob, Alex and Bailey – thank you for making me the luckiest guy on the planet. Thank you Sara, especially, for believing in me and encouraging me to chase my dreams.

Lastly, to those of you reading this, thank you – you're helping me feed my kids!

INTRODUCTION:
Why LinkedIn?

Remember *Indiana Jones and the Raiders of the Lost Ark?* (It will be the first of many 1980s references sprinkled throughout this book, so apologies in advance if you weren't alive back then!) If you haven't seen it, well, you're missing out on one of the all-time great adventure films ever made!

Anyway, the penultimate scene of *Raiders* is when the bad guys – the Nazis – try to open up the Ark of the Covenant, a sacred Christian relic that was used to carry the Ten Commandments along with giving God's armies incredible power, making them invincible in battle. (Thus the reason the Nazis want it so bad in the movie.)

As the Nazis open the Ark, God's power is unleashed and since they are the bad guys, their faces literally melt when they look into it. (If you don't believe me, go Google "Indiana Jones face melting scene" and watch it on YouTube!) Also, one guy's head explodes, but that's not my point here.

My point is this: When I came across the stat I'm about to share with you, I immediately flashed back to that scene from *Raiders of the Lost Ark*. That's why I've coined this as my "Face Melting Stat" during live presentations and talks I give on how vital LinkedIn is to you and your business right now.

Here it is: LinkedIn now accounts for 64 percent[1] of all corporate website traffic that comes via social media channels.

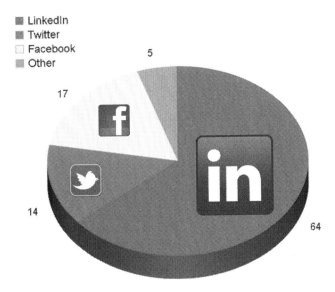

Think about that for a minute: *64 percent of ALL the traffic coming to your corporate or business website from social media channels is coming from LinkedIn!*

Not what you expected, right?

To understand how we got here, you first need to see how much LinkedIn has changed. From its inauspicious beginnings in 2003 as a basic "careers" website with 4,500 users, to a global B2B lead generation and networking phenomenon with nearly 300 million members as of this writing, LinkedIn has become an indispensible social network when it comes to doing business online.

LinkedIn notes that it is adding more than *two new members every second*, meaning the social network is adding about 63 million new members every year. It has users in more than 200 countries worldwide, and is seeing explosive growth in places like Asia, Australia and Europe, to name a few.

The natural question of course, is this: *What in the hell is going on here?*

There are many answers, but I think the simplest one is this: There are no silly cat videos on LinkedIn. Nobody is posting photos of their dogs or kids and talking about what they ate for lunch.

LinkedIn is a *professional* network, meaning people are on there to do one of three things: Find a job, Find an employee or Find someone to do business with.

That's it. By and large, people are on LinkedIn to talk and do business, period. As a result, it's become fertile ground for those of us providing any sort of business-to-business (B2B) type products or services, along with (to a lesser extent) business-to-consumer marketing. And when you see what LinkedIn has in store in terms of content creation and other platform enhancements, you're face really *might* melt as a result!

Bottom line: When it comes to online marketing and social media, *LinkedIn is the single best way to generate the most qualified sales leads in the shortest amount of time.* And it doesn't have to cost you a penny!

How I Made $135,000 in 90 Days on LinkedIn using my MacBook Pro and an empty Super Pretzels Box

I started my own business on November 6, 2012. I remember the date because one of my co-workers at the Minnesota Nurses Association said, "I can't believe Nemo's last day is Election Day! What were you thinking? You can't quit on election day!"

But I did. I remember walking out the back door of the building and clambering down the loud, metallic steps suspended over the asphalt parking lot. A sharp, cold wind whipped me in the face, and I strode toward my car with a mixture of fear and excitement growing in the pit of my stomach.

I had just left the safest job I'd ever known. I was being paid $120,000 a year and had a union contract that meant it was almost impossible to fire me. I also had gold-plated healthcare benefits, plus a union pension fund that I would be eligible for in another few months.

And I quit.

I had three boys at home under the age of 10, and my wife was home full-time raising the kids and running the show. I was the sole income earner in our family, and I'd just quit the safest, most "sure thing" job I'd ever had to start my own marketing agency (Nemo Media Group).

What the hell was I thinking?

A little more than 90 days later, I'd generated more than $135,000 in revenue. All of it came while sitting in our upstairs bedroom, working on a MacBook Pro that was perched atop an empty Super Pretzels box. My desk was a blue folding card table with one wobbly leg. (It still shakes and wiggles whenever my printer runs.)

Despite my humble surroundings, I'd just generated more revenue in 90 days using LinkedIn than I'd made in an entire *year* at my old job!

Even better, I was my own boss. I was getting to do what I loved most – be creative! No more meetings, no more committees, no more wearing pants … okay, I still wore pants, but they were sweatpants! My new "commute" consisted of walking upstairs from the kitchen to our bedroom and firing up my laptop.

And all of it was happening because of one thing…I'd figured out how to leverage LinkedIn like never before. More than 98 percent of the new clients I landed for my business had never met me in real life prior to us connecting on LinkedIn. Yet here they were, giving me $10,000 marketing contracts, $15,000 website contracts and more. I never left the house. I never traveled to trade shows. I never took out expensive advertisements or made cold calls. In fact, I ended up taking inbound calls from people wanting to make a deal while I was out walking the dog!

That first year, I ended up generating almost $300,000 of revenue running Nemo Media Group from my bedroom office.

This book is the story of how I did it, and how you can too.

---

1 "LinkedIn Drives More Traffic to Corporate Websites than other Social Sites," *Social Media Today*, October 21, 2013. URL: http://socialmediatoday.com/steve-rayson/1841146/ linkedin-drives-more-traffic-corporate-websites-all-other-social-sites-combined

CHAPTER 1
Profiles:
Why **99 percent** of people are still using LinkedIn **the wrong way**!

Let me explain.

When LinkedIn started back in 2003, it was little more than a glorified version of Monster.com or other job posting websites. The whole idea was to basically post your résumé online, and maybe an HR person or recruiter would find you. You could also search and apply for jobs through LinkedIn's database. The site also wanted you only connecting with people you already knew in real life. (Think about how much *that* has changed!)

So all of us did what LinkedIn wanted us to – we generated profiles that were all about (wait for it) ... ourselves! We posted our résumés, we talked about where we went to college. We talked about our jobs, industry awards we'd won and more.

We talked about ourselves. Incessantly.

Think about that. We've all been at a cocktail party or social gathering and met a guy who literally never stops talking about himself. We might be trapped in a 10-minute conversation with the clown, and *never once* does he ask us a question about ourselves or how he can help us out.

That's super annoying, right?

Then why do we do the same thing with our LinkedIn profiles?

I hate to break it to you, but outside of your mom, *nobody really cares all that much about what you have to say.* (And your mom probably doesn't either – she's just being polite. She has to. She's your mom.)

You know what other people *do* care about? Themselves!

Dale Carnegie said it best in his book *How to Win Friends and Influence People*: "I know and you know people who blunder through life trying to wigwag other people into becoming interested in them. Of course, it doesn't work. *People are not interested in you. They are not interested in me. They are interested in themselves - morning, noon and after dinner.*"

That's what I mean when I say 99 percent of people are using LinkedIn the wrong way: They've got profiles that *only* talk about themselves.

So what's the solution?

It's simple. If you want to start generating a flood of nonstop sales leads on LinkedIn, you've got to go *Fix-It Felix* on the bit.

Now, if you haven't seen the Disney movie *Wreck-It-Ralph*, it's a hilarious, animated throwback to the glory days of 1980s era video games. If, like me, you grew up during that hilarious decade, you'll instantly be transported back to the days of tube socks pulled up to your knees, short shorts, a fistful of quarters and *Ms. Pac-Man*, *Defender*, and *Donkey Kong* awaiting your best effort at the local video arcade.

Here's the point: *Fix-It Felix* is one of the characters in *Wreck-It-Ralph*. And Felix is beloved by everyone he encounters because if anything breaks ... he fixes it! Armed with a golden hammer, Felix spends his days fixing his customer's problems. (See where I'm going with this?)

Or, as another 1980s icon of eloquence put it: "If you got a problem, yo I'll solve it, now check out the moves while my DJ revolves it!"

Ice, Ice, baby.

Yes, Vanilla Ice was a lyrical poet, and Miami was indeed on the scene in case you didn't know it. But Vanilla and Felix are trying to convey a timeless sales and marketing truth to us: *You must make your LinkedIn profile client facing!*

Because the harsh reality is this: *People care far less about you and your accomplishments than you think.*

With that in mind, I want you to refocus, repurpose and reframe every sentence of your LinkedIn Profile to answer this question: *How does what I'm saying right now help YOU (my ideal client or customer) make more money?*

Every single sentence of your LinkedIn profile should aim to answer these questions: *How does what I'm writing or sharing right now help my clients or customers? How does it solve some of their biggest problems? How does it make their lives easier? How does it make them more money?*

Go to your LinkedIn profile right now, and follow these steps:

STEP 1: Rewrite your professional headline (the profile heading that goes next to your name) so it explains what industry/niche you work in and HOW you help customers or clients in that niche!

John Nemo
LinkedIn Marketing Consultant I LinkedIn Marketing Tips I LinkedIn Lead Generation
Greater Minneapolis-St. Paul Area | Public Relations and Communications

Current   LinkedIn Riches, Nemo Media Group
Previous   Minnesota Nurses Association, ACA International, KTIS-AM Radio
Education   University of Saint Thomas

Edit Profile ▾

500+
connections

IMPORTANT: Before you start, use LinkedIn's Search tool to see what the most popular keyword searches are related to your industry. How are people finding the type of products or services you offer? What search terms are they using? Try to think like your prospects – *If I were in their shoes, what would I punch into LinkedIn Search to find someone offering what we do?*

STEP 2: Edit your Contact Information area's Website and Blog listings. Instead of choosing "Company Website" or "Blog" or one of the other lame default options LinkedIn offers, choose "Other" and then write in a brief phrase addressing a need you meet or a problem you solve. Say something like "How We Help Dentists Get More Patients" or "Media Training Tips" and have the URL point to a page on your blog or website that does exactly that!

> 🌐 Websites   **Free LinkedIn Marketing Tips!**
> **Join my LinkedIn Group!**
> **Debt Collection Marketing Tips**

STEP 3: Next, start off your LinkedIn profile's Summary section with ALL CAPS and create phrases like "WHAT WE DO" or "WHY WE'RE DIFFERENT." LinkedIn doesn't allow bold, italic or other types of text formatting, so ALL CAPS is a great way to make something stand out! Again, note how I want everything in your summary to be client facing.

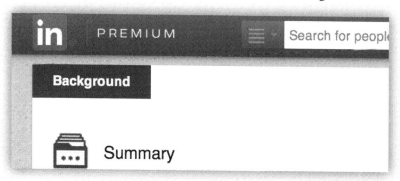

Search for people, jobs, companies, and more...

Background

 Summary

WHAT I DO: I teach people how to leverage LinkedIn to generate nonstop sales leads, add new clients and increase revenue!

WHY IT WORKS: What I've found is that LinkedIn is hands down the BEST platform to quickly and easily generate online leads for your business. I knew I had it figured out when I did more than $135,000 of revenue in just 90 days using LinkedIn! And all of it was for a tiny niche (where I was trying to sell marketing services to Debt Collection Agencies) that nobody would even think of using LinkedIn for to begin with!

HOW IT WORKS: I've distilled everything - all my best secrets, tips and strategies - into a 60-minute online training I called LinkedIn Riches. The simple method I teach you works in any niche, takes just a few minutes a day to apply and will drive targeted, ready-to-buy prospects to your virtual front door. It doesn't matter what your experience level is when it comes to LinkedIn – literally anyone can do this! Plus the course has a TON of FREE bonus material, including 1-on-1 coaching and interviews with industry-leading Marketing, PR and SEO professionals.

There's a lot more info on the main website: http://www.LinkedInRiches.com

VIDEO: LinkedIn Lead Generation - How it Works!   Join my LinkedIn Marketing Tips Group!

 Experience

LinkedIn Marketing Consultant I LinkedIn Marketing Tips I Creator of LinkedIn Riches Online Training

LinkedIn Riches

September 2013 – Present (7 months) I Greater Minneapolis-St. Paul Area

WHAT I OFFER: Discover the exact method I used to do more than $135,000 in revenue in just 90 days using LinkedIn! In less than 60 minutes, you'll unlock the secrets to making money on the world's largest business networking platform.

WHAT OTHERS SAY: "Having personally evaluated and participated in countless courses like this over the past 15 years, I can honestly say John Nemo has created something truly unique with LinkedIn Riches. Anytime you buy a course like this, you want a quick win, and just halfway through the first module, John Nemo made me a believer! I love how this course not only gives you amazing insights, but also provides easy, "how-to" actions you can take immediately with your LinkedIn profile and other areas. Plus, the amazing bonuses John offers in addition to the course are worth the price tag alone! As someone who came into this thinking LinkedIn was a boring, stuffy network that wasn't really worth my time, consider my eyes opened – wide!"
-- John Morgan, Bestselling Marketing Author, Brand Against The Machine

"When it comes to LinkedIn, John Nemo is a marketing genius. His system has brought in dozens of new clients and generated an ongoing stream of qualified sales leads who are looking for exactly the type of services we offer. I can't recommend John and this course enough!"
-- Thomas Backal, Lazarus Financial Group

STEP 4: Add in multimedia clips (videos, online presentations, links to pages on your website, photos or portfolios, etc.) to your Summary section that highlight products or services you offer, and include a client facing caption. Also link to video clips of speeches, media coverage or other items that demonstrate your expertise so you can build credibility with your prospects.

Media clips are a *great* way to capture someone's attention with striking visuals, enticing him or her to want to watch a video or flip through a presentation. Take advantage!

If you don't have any of your own original content to share, LinkedIn makes it easy for you to import videos, presentations, images and online stories from other sources, including leading newspaper websites, so you can still find something relevant and valuable to share on your profile.

Go crazy with this feature! There's no limit on it. Add visual elements to your profile, and make sure each complements the specific job section or summary area that you're placing it in. It's also a great opportunity to offer social proof – client testimonial videos, you speaking on stage and the audience loving you, your media appearances, etc.

STEP 5: Repeat Steps 1, 3 and 4 for every single job you have listed on your LinkedIn profile – edit the job title and summary, then add clips and work samples as well.

Trust me, if you make these changes, prospects are going to find their way to your virtual front door through LinkedIn Search and other avenues. And when they do, they're going to be banging it down, because your profile will be offering them *exactly* what they are looking for!

Your LinkedIn Profile = Home Base

Let me walk you through *exactly* how to set up a killer LinkedIn profile. Don't skip over this section, because I'm going to help you discover how to get your profile ranking #1 overall in *any* industry or niche on LinkedIn!

Think about that for a moment. What if, whenever one of LinkedIn's 300 million plus members went into LinkedIn's huge internal search engine and typed in a certain set of keywords, job titles or phrases related to a product or service you provide, *your* profile showed up at the top of the list! It's like ranking at the top of a Google Search!

Step 1: Your Photo

Before we get to that, however, we've got to make sure we begin with your profile photo. You've got to have a *great* photo. What I mean by that is a professional quality headshot. One where you are smiling, friendly, attractive ... at your best! This is the kind of photo that my wife would let me put online and not be embarrassed by. Not one of the photos of me playing *Star Wars* with my kids, or flexing at the beach *(Hey – anybody want two tickets to the gun show?)*, or playing with my dog, or even my company logo.

Remember: LinkedIn is both a human *and* professional network. We do business with other *people,* so that's why it's important to show your smiling face (in a professional manner) to the masses!

What floors me to this day is (A) People who don't have a LinkedIn photo and (B) Who make sure their profile shows up as "Anonymous" whenever they view someone's profile.

If Your Profile Does This...

LinkedIn member
This member chose to be shown as anonymous

LinkedIn member
This member chose to be shown as anonymous

Prospects Do This...

I mean, that's like walking into a business networking event or cocktail party with a paper bag over your head and a sign around your neck that says, "Please, don't talk to me." What's the point? I still don't get what these LinkedIn lurkers are up to. Having an "anonymous" profile with no photo is a great way to ensure you get ZERO value or business from the platform.

Moving on, another point I can't emphasize enough: Do NOT make your LinkedIn profile photo your company logo! You might be really proud of it, and think it looks cool, or that it's good "branding," but here's the reality – *nobody cares about your company logo!*

We don't do business with logos. I've never shaken a logo's hand or looked it in the eye or talked to it on the phone.

We do business with *people.* I might love Apple's iPhone as a product, but it was *Steve Jobs* who sold it to me via his keynotes. He's the one who made me feel like, "I've got to have an iPhone right now! I can't believe how cool this thing is!" Yes, Apple is a company, but to a large degree, Apple was (and still is) Steve Jobs.

No matter how big or how small, we still do business with *people.*

And on LinkedIn, the first impression people have of you is going to be your profile photo. Immediately, it's going to answer these questions: *What kind of person are you? Are you likable? Trustworthy? Friendly? Is this someone I want to be associated with?*

Fair or not, we all judge a book by its cover, and a picture says a thousand words. There's a reason companies hire well-dressed, attractive sales people to occupy trade show booths. There's a reason TV newscasters use power tools to put on pounds of makeup and never have a hair out of place before going on air.

What's more, psychology has shown that we all instantly make snap judgments when we *see* someone in the room before they've even said a word. We've already made up our mind about you before you even say a word! "The clothes make the man" and all that.

The point: Make sure you have a great profile photo!

Keep in mind, too, with LinkedIn, when you're posting in Groups and on your news feed, it's going to have a small square of your profile photo, and it's much easier to see who that is if it's a head shot versus a faraway group shot or a logo. Again, not to belabor the point (which I just did), but make sure you have a killer photo!

Next up is your overall LinkedIn title that goes next to your pretty face. Your title is *huge*. You want to have a title that is client facing. (Sick of hearing that yet?) *What do you do for people? What problems do you solve? What services do you provide?*

Here are a couple of more reasons why you're LinkedIn title is so important. First, it's important to know that LinkedIn is *very* keyword-specific. If you want to show up #1 on LinkedIn in your niche and industry, *you've got to have a title that uses the same keywords that your prospects use when searching on LinkedIn.* In my case, I want people to find a LinkedIn marketing consultant, or someone looking for LinkedIn marketing tips or training, so that's why those keywords are in my title.

The next thing is to think about what's in your overall summary. As I mentioned earlier, make that all client facing: *Here's what I do. Here are the problems I solve for my clients. Here's why I'm unique/different/better than other people who offer similar services or products. Here's what clients say about working with me.* If you've just landed on my profile via LinkedIn Search and are curious about me, I'm getting right to the nuts and bolts. I'm simplifying for you as a prospect what I do and whether or not you're going to be interested in working with me.

For the love of all things Dale Carnegie, do NOT write your summary like an online résumé! Don't just put in your past work history, like everyone else does. Be creative! Be original! Insert some personality and some panache! (I checked with LinkedIn's corporate headquarters, and they confirmed it is indeed OK to act like a human being on their network.) Make it all about the problems you solve (remember *Fix-It Felix*?) for your customers and how you make their headaches disappear. Mix in the capital letter trick I showed you earlier as well.

Next, I want you to stuff your profile with the type of keywords and search phrases your ideal client or customer would punch into Google to find someone who does what you do. I want you to go Subway mode – make yourself a big old keyword sandwich! Stuff that thing!

Spend some time first with LinkedIn's own Search box, typing in certain types of keywords or phrases that you think people would use to find someone who offers your type of product or service. Once you get a good idea of what those keywords are, put them ALL OVER your profile!

Who's #1?

LinkedIn determines its Search results in two ways: First, it determines your individual search results based on the network of people you are connected to. So, the more people you're connected to in your key industry or niche, the better you'll show up in their search results. (More connections = better shot of showing up high on someone's search results!) Second, LinkedIn Search looks for *keyword density and relevance* when determining whose profile should show up first.

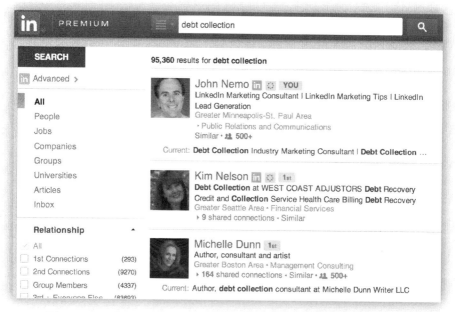

It's not rocket science. First, connect with a *ton* of people in your industry or niche that comprise your ideal clients or customers. (More on how to do that *en masse* later on.) Second, load up your LinkedIn job titles and summary areas with keywords!

John Nemo = Debt Collector?

This works in any niche. If you type in "debt collection" and are within my sphere of 1st, 2nd or 3rd party connections, I'm #1 overall. Which is great, because I started my sales approach on LinkedIn by going *very* niche – I decided to sell marketing services to debt collection agency owners.

Here's why: When I opened up Nemo Media Group for business in late 2012, the best advice I got was to go niche. Instead of trying to be a marketing agency for anybody and everybody, I decided to pick out a specific audience to cater to, and made every single piece of marketing material I created all about how I could help people in the debt collection industry make more money.

It wasn't like I'd decided this on a whim. Before working at the Minnesota Nurses Association, I was the PR Director for ACA International, an international trade association for credit and debt collection professionals. That meant I actually understood how the credit and collection industry worked (giving me an advantage over 99.9 percent of other marketing and PR agencies) and I also knew the people in this industry were being *way* underserved on the marketing side of things.

The constant compliant I heard from debt collectors while at ACA and afterward was that nobody understood them or their industry. They'd hire a website designer or PR firm, but then had to spend more time trying to explain the countless nuances of the heavily regulated Accounts Receivable Management (ARM) industry than it was worth. Inevitably, the outside vendor trying to create press releases or website content just couldn't grasp what to say and how to say it when it came to helping these collection agencies land new clients and add more revenue.

Enter Nemo Media Group!
Now, there were only about 5,000 or so debt collection agencies in the entire United States when I started marketing to them on LinkedIn in November of 2012. (Remember, this was the *sole* audience I was going after with my new business.) And most of these businesses were smaller, "mom and pop"

agencies that didn't have marketing budgets or money to spend on an outside vendor like me.

But I knew there was money to be had, and I knew that almost *all* of these agencies needed marketing help – new websites, marketing videos, logos, content creation, PR services, RFP writing and design … the list went on and on. While many couldn't afford the rates I would charge, I reasoned there had to be plenty that would.

So I set my LinkedIn profile up as *The Debt Collection Marketing Guy*. My entire corporate website (www.NemoMediaGroup.com) was literally all about debt collection marketing. I left no stone unturned. Every piece of content I created – blog posts, sales pages, press releases – talked about *how I helped debt collection agencies add new clients and increase revenue*.

Once I started working my magic on LinkedIn, using the techniques I'm teaching you throughout this book, the dollars started rolling in. Our three boys started calling my laptop "The Money Machine" because I was always shouting after opening up my MacBook Pro to see another signed contract in my email inbox. The U.S. Mail truck also got renamed "The Money Truck" because it was dropping off checks several times a month!

It's important to note that this wasn't some get rich quick scheme. I didn't sit there in my underwear munching on Super Pretzels and magically make money on LinkedIn. I worked my face off. I created and gave away tons of free, high-quality content that was ultra useful and valuable to collection agency owners looking for advice on how to grow their business. I put in my time on LinkedIn, networking like crazy, doing my best not to sell or be pushy but instead to add value and give personalized, free marketing advice to anyone and everyone who asked.

It didn't take long for people to respond, and they quickly started seeking *me* out asking to do business.

LinkedIn Success = Niche Marketing

See the lesson here? Cater to a *specific* niche or segment of people in your industry on LinkedIn, and make your approach *all about them.* How can you meet their biggest needs or solve their most pressing problems with the products or services you offer?

At this point, some of you are throwing up your hands and saying, "Well, what if I cater to people in different industries or niches? Am I supposed to set up 10 different individual LinkedIn profiles to try and do this?"

Put your hands down. Here's what you do: Keep your main LinkedIn profile, and just add in specific "jobs" to cover each industry or niche you serve. With each individual "job" listing and summary you set up, you can load in the keywords and service offerings like I talked about earlier in this chapter. Do it for as many niches as you like.

I do the same thing with my profile. My overall headline and summary is all about my LinkedIn Marketing Tips and services. But I have a keyword loaded job listing for Nemo Media Group that is all about Debt Collection Marketing, and that enables me to still show up #1 overall when people in my network search for "Debt Collection." At the same time, I show up very high when the same people in my network search for "LinkedIn Marketing Consultant" or similar phrases.

Where it Went = Do it for me, too!

Back to my story for a bit. Now that I had become known as the *Debt Collection Marketing Guy* on LinkedIn, the same debt collection agency clients who'd discovered and hired me for marketing projects began asking me to replicate my LinkedIn formula for them. So I did, helping collection agencies and related businesses start leveraging LinkedIn to generate sales leads and add new clients.

One of the many individual success stories is Tyler Parisi, who went through my LinkedIn Riches premium training online. Take a look at Tyler's profile and you'll see how he's got variations of the phrase "debt collection" plastered all over his profile, job titles, etc. It's called "keyword stuffing," and it's a *major* reason he shows up on the first page of LinkedIn Searches in his network for "debt collection."

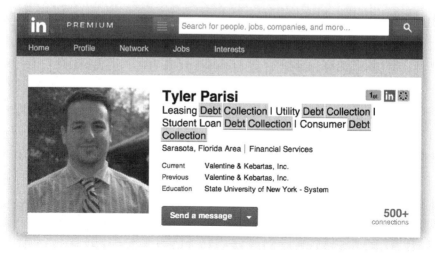

Summary

WHAT WE DO FOR OUR CLIENTS: Valentine & Kebartas, Inc. delivers big agency results while providing small agency attention! Whether it is a BPO project, First Party Collections, Third Party Collections or a Letter Series, we have the technology, training and infrastructure in place to help our clients succeed. We know how critical communication is to successful debt collections, and it's no different with our clients! Our "always available" approach to Client Services means we're always ready to give YOU the service and attention to detail you deserve from a Debt Collection Agency Partner. What we've learned is this: With communication, partnerships last!

VKI'S SALES APPROACH: I attended a debt collection conference and overheard a salesman speaking to a potential client. The salesman's approach was to tell the potential client that his debt collection agency will be #1 on his portfolio and that he'd be crazy not to do business with him.

This approach got me thinking that prospects must be SICK TO DEATH hearing the same "CANNED SALES PITCH" all the time. Am I right?

OUR GOAL is to explore the idea of us becoming your debt collection partner. We do this by finding out what your debt collection needs are and then we develop a collection strategy tailor made to fit them. Wouldn't you rather have a debt collection agency customize their services around your needs rather than expect you to adjust to a cookie-cutter service?

COMPLIANCE: The debt collection industry is very different today compared to when VKI first opened its doors. Today debt collection agencies not only have the FDCPA to comply with but also the CFPB and TCPA. At VKI we have been proactive by developing an internal compliance department and a quality assurance team. We realize that treating our client's delinquent customers with respect by utilizing a customer service approach is just as important to our clients as the amount of money we are able to recover.

Experience

VP of Debt Collection Sales at VKI a Debt Collection Agency
Valentine & Kebartas, Inc.
September 2003 – Present (10 years 7 months) | Sarasota, Florida Area

My responsibility is to develop relationships with individuals in the debt collection world and see if VKI would be a good fit for their collection needs. I really enjoy meeting new people in this industry and have found the best place to do so is at one of the many collections conferences throughout the year. We typically attend PLATTS, CRS, NASP, NE Utility, ELFA and the PDG conferences. If you are interested in meeting please be sure to look me up. At the very least you will make a new friend in the industry.

▾ 5 recommendations, including:

 Joe Adams
Executive Vice President, Hampton Pryo...

 Jack Byrne
Site Director of Operations at The Result...

Tyler is an excellent sales professional that understands the needs of the client come first. His attention to detail is... View↓

I interacted with Tyler during the vetting process to choose vendors to work collections for us. During that time I always... View↓

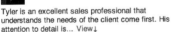

3 more recommendations ↓

Utility Debt Collection I Utility Debt Recovery I Utility Receivables Management

Valentine & Kebartas, Inc.

July 2002 – November 2013 (11 years 5 months) I Lawrence, MA

Valentine & Kebartas, Inc has been helping utility companies with their debt collection needs since 1994. We regularly attend the NE Utility and PLATTS conference to meet new decision makers in the utility arena. Please be sure to contact us If you are in the market for a utility debt collection agency.

Leasing Debt Collection I Leasing Debt Recovery I Leasing Receivables Management

Valentine & Kebartas, Inc.

May 2001 – November 2013 (12 years 7 months) I Sarasota, Florida Area

VKI has been helping consumer and commercial leasing companies with their debt collection needs since 1996. Some of the companies that we have partnered with are Dell Financial Services, GE, Fifth Third Leasing and Wells Fargo Equipment Finance. Please let me know if you are interested in VKI helping you with your leasing debt collection needs.

See how easy this is?

Now, an important caveat about keyword stuffing: If you look at my profile, it still reads well. It's still relevant and makes sense. What I mean by this is that you should NOT just copy and paste the phrase "debt collection" or whatever else onto your profile 100 times and then dislocate a shoulder patting yourself on the back for a job well done.

You still have to create a LinkedIn profile that reads well and (most importantly) is *all about the headaches and problems you solve for your clients through your specific product or service.*

LinkedIn Profile URLs = Free Advertising!

One of the next steps I want you to take with your profile is to edit your public URL.

It's easy to customize your public profile URL on LinkedIn. You can change it to whatever you want. But if you don't change it, you just get a generic bunch of letters and numbers. You want to change it to something that either has your full name or something clever like, "HireJohnNemo" or "B2BMarketingTips" – whatever you want to do. Change that and save it. That's a simple, fast way to improve your profile, and also another way people can easily remember how to find you on LinkedIn.

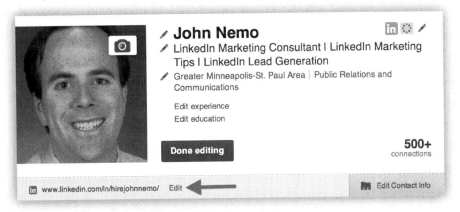

Recommendations = Gold, Baby! Gold!

Another area to focus on with your individual profile is LinkedIn Recommendations. You can literally never get enough recommendations, i.e. customer testimonials. I can't say this enough: *Recommendations are gold!*

Every business owner knows that getting someone else recommending our business is *way* more effective than us trying to tell you (the customer) how great we are.

When it comes to your LinkedIn profile, don't just claim authority. Instead, let your happy clients and customers do it for you!

LinkedIn makes it easy to ask one of your connections to recommend you. The key (as with almost everything on LinkedIn) is to *personalize* your "ask" to each specific individual you want a testimonial from.

If you don't, LinkedIn will immediately just go right to that person and say, "Hey, John wants you to recommend him. Do you want to do that?" Make sure that before you send the request, you include a personal note explaining to the person *why* you're asking for this.

For example: "Hi Joe, I'm trying to boost my presence on LinkedIn, and I know you said you were thrilled with [service or product XYZ] when we did business together at [Company XYZ.] I was hoping you might have a minute to put that in writing for me here on LinkedIn. I'd be beyond grateful if you could!"

If you don't already have a ton of recommendations, go through your connections and happy customers and ASK FOR THEM!

You can also jumpstart the process by giving an unsolicited testimonial to someone else first. If you do this, (A) They will be thrilled and flattered and (B) They will feel socially obligated to return the favor, which LinkedIn makes it easy to do whenever you accept someone else's recommendation.

Remember, nothing beats this type of social proof from real human beings. With LinkedIn, each testimonial includes real names, photos, profiles, etc., so it carries a lot more weight than testimonials like, "Dentist, Topeka, Kansas" or "Joseph, Aviation Executive." Anybody can (and some probably do!)

make up testimonials that lack a full name, photo, job title or company name. It's much more believable when a *real* person's name, photo and everything else is attached to the testimonial!

Bonus Tip: Double Dip!

While it's great to have people praising your work on your LinkedIn profile, very few people are going to see it compared to the amount of visitors you get to your company website.

So why not double your pleasure?

Here's a tip that literally takes about 5 seconds. First, go to your LinkedIn profile, find your recommendations, and then snap a screen shot of them. Next, jump on your website, and insert the screen shot image of your LinkedIn recommendations onto whatever pages you want to.

BOOM! Instant credibility, and best of all, you've got recommendations from REAL PEOPLE, complete with names, photos, job titles, companies, etc. Since these testimonials are already displayed on your public LinkedIn profile, there's no reason you can't copy and paste them onto your main website as well, right?

Skills & Expertise = Phony, but it matters!

One final area that I want to touch on with your LinkedIn profile is the skills and expertise section. It's a little bit of a game. I get these endorsements all the time from people I don't even know I'm connected to. I've got thousands of connections, so randomly people will say, "Yeah, I endorse John for blogging!"

I want to reply, "Dude, you've never even *read* my blog, how could you know I'm good at that?"

I think in general, the LinkedIn community looks at this part of our profiles with deserved skepticism, so don't focus on this part of your profile a whole lot.

With that said, it *is* important to make sure you've added the "Expertise and Skills" keywords or items that you *want* to be known for, and (most important) the ones that you think your clients and customers will be searching for or measuring you by.

Honors and Awards = Everybody's Got a Trophy

Honors and Awards is another profile area I'll touch on. Typically, it's pretty buried on your LinkedIn profile. You can move it up to the top, but honestly, nobody really cares about your honors and awards. Instead, they care about ... *Paging Dale Carnegie! Mr. Carnegie, we need you over here again!*

> "I know and you know people who blunder through life trying to wigwag other people into becoming interested in them. Of course, it doesn't work. People are not interested in you. They are not interested in me. They are interested in themselves - morning, noon and after dinner."
> – *Dale Carnegie*

CHAPTER 2

Prospects:

How to **instantly locate** your **ideal customers** on LinkedIn no matter what **industry you're in**!

OK, so you're individual profile is all pimped out. Now what?

If you don't get busy bringing prospects to your virtual front door, all that work you just did on your profile is for nothing. It's like building a mansion in the middle of the woods but forgetting to add a road. How the heck is anybody going to find you if you don't give them directions?

LinkedIn and Lead Generation – It's the Groups, Stupid!

Students of political history will remember strategist James Carville's famous mantra that helped Bill Clinton win the 1992 U.S. presidential campaign: "It's the economy, stupid!"

In the case of finding, engaging and connecting with your ideal prospects on LinkedIn, "It's the Groups, stupid!"

The fastest – and easiest – way to start paving that road for your ideal prospects or customers to find you on is through LinkedIn's 2.1 million professional Groups.

In case you're not familiar, LinkedIn's Groups are one of its most powerful and popular features. There is literally a Group for everyone and everything. Best of all, LinkedIn does all the work for you, gathering all the prospects you want to reach in a specific niche or industry in one place – their Group!

Say you want to sell a product to Veterinarians. There are literally thousands of DVMs hanging out in scores of LinkedIn Groups. Say you need to reach Debt Collection Agency Executives. I landed almost all of my clients early on by mining just *one* LinkedIn Group filled with thousands of credit and collection execs. If it's an industry with professionals, there are LinkedIn Groups with thousands of those professionals hanging out inside it.

Granted, LinkedIn Groups have become inundated with self-serving sales pitches and spam (more on that later), but for now you don't need to worry about that. Instead, you're going to start finding your proverbial fish in a barrel!

The Plan of Attack

First, you'll want to join as many Groups as you can (LinkedIn allows you to join a maximum of 50) in your particular niche or industry. (Note: The more "niche" you can get here, the better.)

Once you get accepted into an individual Group that is filled with your ideal customers and prospects, go to its "Members" page. You'll notice all the members of the Group listed, and here's the really cool part – you can further filter your search of those members by job title, physical location or other criteria.

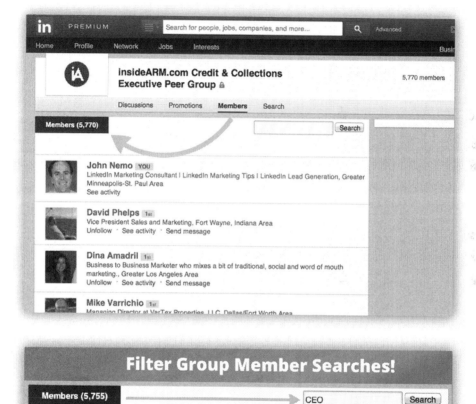

Boom! Once you run a filtered search, you'll instantly create a list of ready-made prospects based on specific job titles, company names, physical locations or any other criteria you want to sort by.

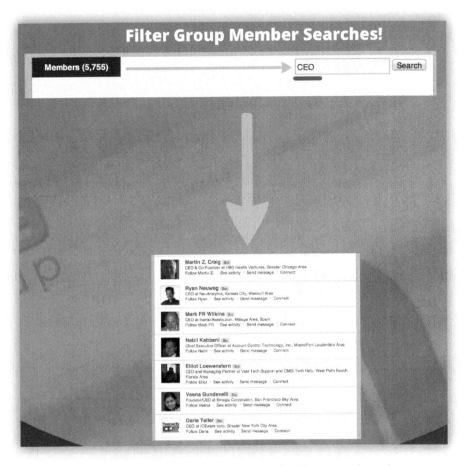

How cool is that? You didn't spend a dime, and you've got a list of your ideal prospects sitting right in front of your eyes! No gatekeepers, no middle management…you get to go straight to the decision makers!

Think about it. Say you need to sell dental office supplies to dentistry clinics in Atlanta. You join a Dental Group with 5,000 members, get accepted, and then go to the "Members" page. You filter your search by "Atlanta," and LinkedIn instantly pulls up a list of all Group members (i.e., Dentists and dental office managers) who work in Atlanta!

In the next chapter, I'm going to show you what may be *the* most important thing about leveraging LinkedIn to generate leads and sales – how to engage with people!

CHAPTER 3

Personality:
How to **engage** your ideal **prospects** on LinkedIn by creating instant **likability and trust**!

Once you've built your list of ideal prospects inside an individual Group, it's time to start connecting!

I suggest starting with a personalized invitation to connect. One of the biggest mistakes I *still* see people making on LinkedIn is not taking the time to send a personalized invitation. Just trying to bang through the generic "I'd like to add you to my professional network" LinkedIn invites is not only ineffective and lazy, but it can also lead to you getting flagged as a spammer, which then restricts your ability to send people invites in the future.

Here's a simple way to personalize an invite that takes all of about 14 seconds to execute. Open up the profile of the person you want to connect with in a new tab, and scan his

Education

University of Alabama
BS, Marketing
1969 – 1973

Activities and Societies: Tau Epsilon Phi

University of Florida
business marketing
1969 – 1970

Activities and Societies: Tau Epsilon Phi

Mountain Brook High School
1967 – 1969

 Organizations

Additional Organizations

Better Business Bureau, American Collectors Association, International, Birmingham Area Chamber
Commerce, Vision Benchmark group, Jewish Community Center, National Speakers Association

 Additional Info

Interests

golf, jogging, tennis, University of Alabama sports

Personal Details

Birthday   November 5
Marital Status   Married

or her profile. Look for something personal to mention in your invitation. Where did he or she go to college? What city does this person live in? Does he or she have any hobbies or volunteer organizations or causes listed?

I love mentioning something NOT related to work in my LinkedIn invites. First, people aren't expecting it, and it makes my invite stand out because it's so different. Second, when I ask someone about his or her hobbies, passions and interests outside of work, it helps build a relationship and context around something important to them, which again helps me stand out in their memory. It also paves the way for future messages as a friendly, non-work theme I can weave into each one.

How a 60 second YouTube Video got me a $10,000 marketing contract

One of my favorite examples of this involves what I call "Send it in, Jerome!"

Here's the story: I came across the profile of a debt collection agency executive I wanted to connect with and (hopefully) sell some of my marketing services to at some point in the future.

Before I invited him to connect, I spent about 14 second looking over his LinkedIn profile. I noticed he went to University of Pittsburgh and graduated during the 1980s a *huge* sports fan, and I remember the Pitt Panthers great in football (with Dan Marino) in the early 198 Pitt also having a nice run in college hoops during the late 1980s with Jerome Lane, Sean Miller, Charles S others. And of course, the seminal moment in Pit basketball history also happened during the 1980s

"Send it in, Jerome! Send it in!"

It was a home game, and Pittsburgh got a rebound and moved down the court on a fast break. Sean Miller, the Panthers' point guard, dribbled toward the other team's basket while his tall, athletic teammate Jerome Lane streaked down the sideline.

Miller fed his teammate a pass in perfect stride. And Jerome Lane took the ball, skied toward the rim and threw down such a thunderous dunk that the glass backboard literally exploded into thousands of tiny shards!

The whole arena went bonkers – I swear my TV screen started shaking from the vibrations inside that building – and longtime TV color commentator Bill Rafferty shouted what would became one of his most famous exclamations: "Send it ، Jerome! Send it in!"

ι don't see *that* happen every day. So, even though I was ٦o at the time, I've always remembered "Send it in,

١rd about 25 years later. I was reaching out to this kedIn who had attended Pittsburgh during these 1980s. As a result, I decided to personalize ٦ up the Pittsburgh sports angle. Keep in ٦ if this guy was a sports fan or not – I a shot trying to connect a passion of ' of his story (his time as a student

ds
the
. I'm
being
٥s, and
mid-to-
٦mith and
٦ Panthers

` this prospect's profile and ٦ear instant response from

the guy: *Oh, man, you brought back the memories! I actually played varsity soccer at Pitt, and Dan Marino was one of the guys who helped recruit me on my campus visit! And hey, I was curious, so I looked at your profile, and we actually are looking for someone to help us market our collection agency. When do you have time for a call?*

I responded back with the times I was available for a call, and then ended my note with, "Okay, I have to ask, given the years you were at Pitt, do you remember THIS?" And then I pasted in a link to the YouTube video of "Send it in, Jerome!"

Again, I got a reply right away: *I was at that game! You can't believe what it was like inside the arena! The whole place was shaking. Oh man, what a memory. And hey, let's talk at 9:30 a.m. on Thursday. Can't wait!*

A couple of phone calls later, I had $10,000 in business secured. Months later, I was doing an internal survey of clients to find out why they'd chosen Nemo Media Group. When I got to this client, he told me it wasn't my website, sales pages or marketing materials that sold him on us.

"You want to know what it was?" he told me. "Honestly, it was, 'Send it in, Jerome!' Man, I must have shared that video with everybody at the office. I just knew we'd hit it off, that you'd be a fun guy to work with, and you obviously knew how to personalize your marketing messages. Everybody was really impressed."

If you get nothing else from this story (other than a classic college basketball highlight), REMEMBER THIS: *We want to do business with people we know, like and trust.*

Let me repeat that: *We want to do business with people we know, like and trust.*

By doing 14 seconds of research and trying to appeal to a personal, non-work passion of my LinkedIn prospect, I landed a $10,000 marketing contract. It's no different than how vendors work the room at trade shows and open bars and parties.

At the end of the day, we are still *human* creatures. We still gravitate toward choosing people we know, like and trust to do business with. Even if they don't have the flashiest product or the best pricing, there is a *relationship* there. Also, it's much harder to stop doing business with someone you consider a friend than it is with a cell phone company that routes you to a call center in India every time you need customer service.

Relationships matter. And I can't think of a faster and easier way to scale that 1-to-1, humanized marketing approach than on LinkedIn. Getting to know my clients, and actually caring about them as human beings is not only good for business, but it's also the right way to live my life. Wouldn't you agree?

Transparency on LinkedIn = Going "Dr. Phil" vs. Being Human

Okay, dear reader, here goes: *I'm not perfect.* I come from a dysfunctional family. I take medication for depression and anxiety. I've struggled with overeating and excess weight for most of my life.

And when I disclose this to clients and customers ... it often leads to some of the highest quality, longest-lasting and most lucrative business relationships I've ever had!

Here's why: When I risk the *right* amount of vulnerability, transparency and honesty in dealing with clients and prospects, it offers up an important opportunity to bond that goes beyond doing business together. It also helps people to know, like and trust me.

Now, notice I said "the right amount" of sharing. Because if you approach a client call or interaction like an episode of *Oprah* or *Dr. Phil,* cutting open a vein about your life issues, you will turn people off in a hurry and scare them away. I always try to err on the side of being honest or vulnerable without being dramatic or going into gory detail.

Also, it doesn't have to be heavy issues. For example, since I work from home, I'm often in the midst of madness with our three young boys and Rosie the dog running around. My biggest client called the other day and started the conversion with, "What are you up to right now, John?"

"Well, I'm sitting at the kitchen table helping my five-year-old write a story about a talking penguin for his homework assignment," I said, laughing. "You asked what I was doing right now, so..."

Now, I know this client has a couple of young kids, so he can relate to *exactly* what I'm talking about. I probably wouldn't have said the same thing to a client without a family or young kids, but you get the idea.

It might feel like a HUGE risk to take this approach in how you do business and interact with clients. (And to some degree it is!) But what I've found is that doing this actually *attracts* the type of people I want to work with as clients, and it builds long-lasting, lucrative business relationships as a result.

So what does all of this have to do with generating leads and using LinkedIn to do business? Everything! Remember, LinkedIn is a *social* network, and I can't put into words how important humanized, 1-on-1 marketing is when it comes to LinkedIn.

So how about it? Are you willing to insert more of who you REALLY are into your dealings with clients and prospects? Why or why not?

What my dog can teach you about interacting on LinkedIn

Let's take another approach. Rosie is our 1-year-old Wheaten Terrier, and when I watch her operate, I can't help but see how "most" of her behavior is the perfect illustration for how to successfully use LinkedIn for business.

I say "most" because I don't think chewing shoes or licking strangers' faces will endear you to prospects and new connections on LinkedIn. Then again…

But seriously, close your eyes and think about your favorite dog. *What do you love most about him or her?* And if you're not a "dog person," then just play along for a minute.

Here's what I love about our dog:

Her Personality. She's always happy to see you, no matter what the rest of the world thinks or has told you. She's always ready to engage and brighten your day.

Her Unselfishness. Dogs are always giving – love, affection, interaction, play, intimacy, entertainment. Cats are takers and manipulators. (Sorry cat people, but you know it's true. Your cat *owns* you!) Dogs are givers – they're always bringing some sort of value or benefit into your day.

Her Ability to Read People. Our dog seems to have this innate ability to understand or "read" people - *Why doesn't this new person like me? Maybe if I jump on her and lick her face I'll win her over!*

Her Willingness to Ask. When the time is right, I'll get a nudge or a polite whine or even a playful bark. *Can we go on a walk? Can I have some of that pizza? Will you play tug-of-war with me?* Rosie has a way of asking that isn't intrusive, annoying or inappropriate – she seems able to read situations and settings and then adjusts her "ask" accordingly.

Her Transparency. Our dog is … well, a dog. She sniffs poop and pees right in front of you. She doesn't try to pretend she's something she's not or have a hidden agenda. She keeps it pretty simple, and it's refreshing.

Think about all the attributes I just outlined above: *Personality. Unselfishness. Reading Others. Willingness to Ask* (when the time is right). *Transparency.*

If you can display all (or even some) of these traits in how you approach and interact with prospects on LinkedIn, you're going to have massive success. For instance, the ability to "read" your prospects helps you understand what to engage them about and how to engage them. And the willingness to make an "ask" at the right time makes all the difference when it comes to converting a lead into a customer.

The Secret to Successful LinkedIn Invites

I think you'll agree with me on this one: A huge pet peeve of mine is getting the generic "I'd like to add you to my professional network" invites from someone I don't know on LinkedIn.

Why doesn't LinkedIn just change the text to, "I'm too lazy to take five seconds to personalize this, let alone explain how and why we should connect, so just accept my invite so I can pillage your profile and annoy all your hard-earned contacts. Thanks!"

Please don't be *that guy*.

Instead, personalize your invites in the different ways I've already outlined. Plus, remember the three keys to a successful LinkedIn invite:

1. How I Found You. This is really easy if you're connecting through LinkedIn Groups – it gives you an option to choose "Groups" as the way you know this person. That immediately gives them context as to how you found them.

2. Why We Should Connect. Again, what's in it for the other person? Why should they connect with you? What do you have to offer them? What problems can you solve or headaches can you make go away?

3. The Ask – Join my Group! The easy answer to Tip #2 is to create a unique LinkedIn Group (which I'll show you how to do later on) that is all about solving your ideal client or customer's most pressing problems.

Connecting with Collectors

Back to my story: When I wanted to connect with all these

debt collection agency executives who didn't know me, I had a natural "value" *and* "ask" built into the invite:

"Hi Joe – Would love to connect + invite you to my new LinkedIn Group on Debt Collection Agency Marketing Tips. Think you'll find the posts/info really helpful, plus we'd LOVE to have your insights and input to add to the mix. Thanks! – John Nemo"

Note that a little *flattery* doesn't hurt, either! Also in the sample invite above I used some shorthand and symbols. That's because LinkedIn limits how long invites can be. Every character is precious, so cut the fluff and get to the good stuff!

Let's take this invite a step further, and add a personalized tone. Say "Joe" lives and works in Green Bay, Wisconsin. Pretty much everyone who lives in Wisconsin worships the state's professional football team, the Green Bay Packers.

Just writing that last sentence makes me want to puke. I live in Minnesota and *hate* the Packers. Our state's professional football team, the Minnesota Vikings, are bitter rivals with the Packers, and the only thing I like better than seeing the Vikings win is seeing the Packers lose.

Again, tapping into *my* passion for sports, I'm going to personalize "Joe's" invite based on the fact that he lives in the belly of the beast – Green Bay!

Here's a more personalized invite:

"Joe – Against my better professional judgment, I'm going to reach out even though I suspect you're likely a Packers fan! On the non-NFL front, I'd love to connect + invite you to my new

LinkedIn Group on Debt Collection Agency Marketing Tips. I think you'd find the posts/discussions valuable to helping grow your agency, and I know our members would benefit from your insight and input as well. Thanks! – John Nemo"

See what I did there? Sure, I don't *really* know if Joe is a huge Packers fan, but I guarantee you that living in Green Bay means he has an opinion – one way or another – on the Packers. I've immediately made my invite stand out from all the others he gets, and tweaked his curiosity to think, "Who the heck is this guy?" I promise you that Joe is going to go look at my profile *right away* to figure out what my deal is. And once he lands there, he'll see how I'm all about helping collection agencies like his add more revenue and grow their business.

Not only is he likely to accept my invite, but he's also very likely to join my LinkedIn Group as well. In the span of a few seconds, I've just moved Joe halfway down my LinkedIn sales funnel! He went from stranger to connection to member of my LinkedIn Group, where he'll see me repeatedly sharing valuable content and insights that ensure I'm somebody he wants to pay attention to.

How to go "Beast Mode" on LinkedIn Invitations

One of my 10-year-old son Jacob's favorite NFL players is running back Marshawn Lynch, better known by his nickname of "Beast Mode." Lynch earned the moniker because of his aggressive running style, when he goes into "Beast Mode" and starts plowing through defenders one after another. With that in mind, I'm going to show you right now how to go "Beast Mode" with your LinkedIn invitations!

Let's stick with the basic template of what we shared in our personalized invite to "Joe" in Green Bay.

Remember, I'm on the "Members" page of a specific LinkedIn Group right now, starting at a screen of my ideal prospects that I created with LinkedIn's search filter. And here my prospective clients and customers are, all lined up in a nice, neat row, just waiting for me to connect with them!

So what I do after I invite Joe is go to the next person on my list. I paste in the generic part of my invite: "I'd love to connect + invite you to my LinkedIn Group on Debt Collection Marketing Tips…" to start with.

Then I simply open up the next person's profile in a new tab or window and look for something to personalize my invite with. Once I find that, I go back to the invite and "top off" the text I'd already pasted in with my personalized note at the front of the invite.

This takes me probably 60-90 seconds. Then, I'm onto the next prospect. See how fast you can bang through invites this way and *still* make them personalized?

Beast Mode, indeed!

I'll give you a couple more examples of how to do this based on the "Joe" from Green Bay invite.

Let's say the next person after "Joe" is "Jane", a debt collection agency CEO who went to the University of Michigan and is a member of several Michigan alumni Groups that display on her public page. My invite to her would look like this:

"Jane – I have to ask, is the campus atmosphere for UM football REALLY as good as it looks on TV? Always been curious about the Big House! Meantime, I'd love to connect + invite you to my new LinkedIn Group on Debt Collection Agency Marketing Tips. I think you'd find the posts/discussions valuable to helping grow your agency, and we'd love your insight/input as well! Thanks! -John Nemo"

Then I'm onto the next person on my list. See how it works? Within 10 or 20 minutes I can crank through a dozen or more personalized invites! And people LOVE getting invites like these, because I'm starting off the connection by getting them talking about what they love: *Where they went to college, where they live, a favorite sports team or hobby, etc.*

This is why I love LinkedIn: It literally does our job for us as marketers and sales people. In the past, I would have had to meet you in person and start asking you a bunch of questions: "Where are you from? Are you a big fan of the Packers? Where did you go to college? Are you a big fan of golf? Where do you like to volunteer?" Worse, I'd have to *remember* it all! I'd have to take notes on each person I met at that networking event or mixer, and try to remember ways to do personal engagement the next time I had a reason to talk with them.

Instead, LinkedIn literally does it all for me: *Here's Joe. Here's where he works. Here's where he lives. Here's where he went to college. Here are his hobbies and interests. Here are people you have in common and both 'know' via LinkedIn.*

Sure, it's kind of Big Brother, but LinkedIn has made our job as marketers and salespeople infinitely easier as a result.

Are you starting to sense the power this network can provide you when it comes to engaging with your ideal clients and customers?

CHAPTER 4

Profits:
How to turn **LinkedIn Groups** into your own personal **ATM Machine!**

Listen – by the time I'm done with you, you're *literally* going to be going into these groups and pulling money out for your business! I know it sounds crazy, but trust me it when I say it works!

The first thing you need to do is create your own LinkedIn Group. Think of it like your own personal fishing pond that you stock with all of your best prospects. It's going to be a key part of your LinkedIn sales funnel, and it's also going to be a foolproof way for you to generate new business.

You're going to be like those kids at the carnival who go "fishing" in the little toy pool for rubber ducks – because you've stocked the pool with so many ready-to-buy prospects, you can't lose! You catch a fish every time you put your pole in.

Your Group Title = Value + Benefit

When you set up your Group, make sure it is "branded" with your company imagery, logo, etc. LinkedIn will walk you through how to upload banner or "hero" images along with the exact sizes of your logo image and thumbnail images, etc.

Now, this next part is so important I NEED TO WRITE IN ALL CAPS: *Your Group Name should NOT be your company name!*

Instead, the name of your LinkedIn Group needs to convey a specific value + benefit that people will get from joining the Group.

For instance, when I wanted to create my own personal LinkedIn fishing pond/Group and stock it with debt collection agency executives, I did NOT name the Group after myself. I *did* use my Nemo Media Group logo and imagery, but I named the Group "Debt Collection Agency Marketing Tips: More Revenue. More Clients."

You know why? Because debt collection agency executives don't care about my marketing agency or me.

You know what they DO care about? Getting more clients and more revenue.

So what's going to catch their attention more? A LinkedIn Group that says, "Nemo Media Group" or one that says, "Debt Collection Agency Marketing Tips: More Clients. More Revenue"?

Remember, your Group name has to give people an immediate value + benefit of why they should join. And the more you can niche this thing, the better!

Here's an example. Say you sell video marketing services to small business owners, and you've noticed that a lot of your clients lately happen to be veterinary clinics. Sure, you could start a LinkedIn Group that's called "Video Marketing Tips for Small Business Owners," and probably attract people that way. But did you know that LinkedIn allows you to create and manage up to 10 of your own Groups? Why not create another one that's called "Video Marketing Tips for Veterinary Clinics"? Or, even better and more insanely specific, create one that's called "How Veterinary Clinics Can Leverage Video for More Patients + Revenue."

Value + Benefit.

I cannot emphasize this enough! I want you to stop reading this book, hop on Google and find a tattoo parlor nearby. Then go get the words "Value + Benefit" tattooed backward across your forehead. That way, when you wake up every morning and look in the mirror, you'll remember how important it is to give your customers and clients those two things when it comes to leveraging LinkedIn Groups!

I realize it might cause some marital friction, or that your kids might be like, "Dad why do you have those words written backward on your forehead?" You might even feel like the guy in the movie *Memento* who kept tattooing clues and notes all over his body.

I don't care! It's *that* important. Have the tattoo artist add "client facing" on your palms while you're at it.

And if anybody asks why you mutilated your body with marketing slogans, just reply, "Nemo told me to."

I got your back!

Also, this goes beyond LinkedIn. I don't care what it is – your business website, your About Us page … everything you have online needs to talk about the value or the benefit that you bring to your clients, your customers and your prospects.

More on Groups

Once you have your Group name, make sure the Group Description does the same type of thing. "This Group is all about sharing high-value content aimed at helping [Audience XYZ] leverage [Tactics XYZ] to achieve [Outcome XYZ]."

Here's an example.

Group name: Debt Collection Marketing Tips: More Clients. More Revenue.

Group description: "This Group is all about helping debt collection agency owners and executives leverage video, social media, Public Relations and other marketing methods to add new clients, increase revenue and improve and enhance their reputation."

And oh, by the way – the specific tactics, strategies and tips being shared inside your LinkedIn Group will also just happen to be the things YOU do better than anybody else! (More on how that works later.)

Set it up!

When it comes to the Group settings, you want to have it as "request to join." That means you (or someone whom you make a Group Manager) must personally approve everyone who joins.

If you do NOT choose this option, and instead just have a Group that anybody and their grandmother can auto-join, you'll be letting the sharks (competitors) start swimming with all those plump and juicy prospects you've worked so hard to stock your Group with! Tell these jokers and their grandmothers to hold up at the front door! Nobody gets in unless YOU let him or her in!

The same is true with comments and posts. You need to approve everything (at least early on) to make sure people aren't spamming your audience with blatant sales pitches or off-topic discussions.

Remember, you want to keep your Group's waters pure, and the best way to do that is by going all "Mother Russia" on it (another 1980s reference, yes!) by pulling a USSR. You need to rule your Group with an iron fist!

You will also need to work hard – at least in the beginning. That's because you have to build your LinkedIn Group up brick-by-brick. There are no shortcuts. But the good news is this – once you hit a "tipping point" of a few hundred members, your Group will start organically attracting and funneling leads into it. You'll still get to control and get to approve each person who joins, but *they* will be coming to *you!*

The reason is, once your Group gets big enough (usually with a few hundred members), it starts showing up all over people's news feeds. Meaning a prospect you're not connected to in any form or fashion might see something like this show up in his feed: "Joe Smith just joined a Group – Debt Collection Marketing Tips: More Revenue. More Clients." Or maybe it reads like this: "Joe Smith just commented on a post in the Group – Debt Collection Marketing: More Revenue. More Clients."

The bigger your Group is, and the more active its members are, the more mentions of your Group will start showing up all over LinkedIn. Your Group will also start appearing higher in organic Search results, plus people will also see it popping up in their news feeds when a random connection does something inside your Group.

Remember – that one Debt Collector you've connected with and funneled into your Group has about 250 other debt collectors as connections, so it's easy to see how your Group will be of massive interest to those folks when they see something in their news feed that mentions it!

Again, this is why the *name* of your Group is so important! It must capture their curiosity and imply an immediate value + benefit for becoming a member.

Group Invites = Experiment

So the process is pretty simple. As I've outlined earlier, you first go into *other* LinkedIn Groups to find your ideal prospects. Then, you connect with them one-by-one, and *after* they accept your invitation, you invite them (as promised via your original invite text) to join your Group!

You can do this a few different ways, and I suggest experimenting to see what works best. LinkedIn gives you two different options right inside the Group as far as sending out invites. The first, which can be accessed via the little "Share" arrow on the top right corner of your Group home page, allows you to personalize the invite, which I always think is best. But the downside is that it still requires a person to first click on the Group link from your invite message, then go inside the actual Group and click the "Join" button after that.

The second option, under the "Manage" feature of your LinkedIn Group, allows you to blast out a generic invite ("John Nemo would like to invite you to his Group, Debt Collection Marketing Tips") to tons of contacts at once. I do NOT like this approach because I don't get to personalize the invite, but I DO like the fact that this method sends a direct LinkedIn message to the person with a "Join Group" button right inside the message. It makes it easier/faster for the person to join that way.

You can also individually contact people 1-on-1 via LinkedIn Messages with a link to the Group and a personal message asking them to join. Or you can export all your LinkedIn connections into an Excel spreadsheet and then email those people 1-on-1 or as a Group with an email invite to the Group that includes a link or graphic/button that takes them to the Group page.

Experiment and see what works best for you. In my experience, the key is timing and speed. For example, if you get a LinkedIn notification that someone just accepted your original invite to connect, *immediately* send him or her an invite to the Group as your next move.

Keeping Track = Spreadsheets

Look, this can get messy in a hurry. So sometimes it makes sense to create a spreadsheet in a program like Microsoft Excel to track the individual connection invites you've sent, who has or has not accepted, and then the Group invites you've sent to each individual and the result. If you want to get super nerdy, you can even log the date of each communication and the type of Group invite you sent to see which approach is working best.

Why use spreadsheets? The reason is this: LinkedIn does *not* currently do a good job of helping you track all these things. You are able inside your "Sent" folder to track previous individual invites, which is helpful. But there's not a simple way to track what people have accepted your Group invites. You can see inside your Group's "Manage" feature the individuals you've sent invites out to, but you can't easily see in that same area which of those people has accepted/joined the Group.

(Shakes fist at LinkedIn!)

The last thing I want to point out when setting up your Group is to make sure you list it as an "Open" Group. What that means is that yes, you still get to approve everyone *before* they can join, comment or post discussions, but because your Group is "open" anybody can walk by and check out what's going on inside.

Having an "Open" Group is kind of like having a store on Main Street with a big display window. Everyone is walking by on these virtual LinkedIn streets, and when they walk by they might look in your window and check your group out. That means they can see what discussions are going on, what the topics are and whether or not those items would be of interest or value to them. That's a good thing, because you don't want to limit the amount of people that can see your group and see your discussions!

Hero Image = Prime Real Estate!

You'll notice on the main page of your Group a big banner that rotates through various images or certain posts. It's basically a giant billboard, and you can post anything you want on it. LinkedIn lets you insert a giant "hero image" that can have your company logo/branding, and you can also feature certain posts inside the Group as "Manager's Choice" discussions that show up in the billboard area.

This is prime real estate for your best content! Make sure you feature the discussions that you want people to see. You can also use it to promote things like an upcoming webinar or event that your audience would be interested in.

Another powerful feature inside your LinkedIn Group is the ability to "Send an Announcement." You'll find this under the "Manage" feature once you're logged in as the Group Owner or Manager.

The Announcement feature lets you blast message *everyone* in the Group via email, unless they've specifically opted out ahead of time from receiving Group Announcement messages. You can send out this blast message to everyone in the Group once every seven days, and not only does it go into everyone's personal email at home or work, but it also shows up as a post inside the Group. It's a great opportunity to recap specific discussions or pieces of content you want to talk about from the previous week, share news about the Group, highlight an upcoming event or promotion, or even to "sell" the space to people who want to advertise to your Group. You've built the platform and the audience, and if your Group is big enough and targeted enough, advertisers will jump at the chance to reach them via email with a special offer or invitation.

Best of all, the "Send an Announcement" feature lets you include hyperlinks, so you can put links to your website, blog, webinar signup page or whatever else right into the message.

Be careful about how you use this, and don't just blatantly spam people with sales offers. Remember, you've always got to be adding some type of value or benefit to the equation. The same approach should hold true for any advertisers you bring on as well!

More LinkedIn Group Tips & Tricks

I'm going to share later on all about what type of content to create and share inside your Groups, so don't worry about that right now.

However, I would suggest taking advantage of the "Templates" feature inside your Group in the "Manage" area. The most powerful template you can set up is an auto-responder message that people get emailed to them once they join the Group.

I love using this to welcome people to the Group, tell them what to expect, and then include a link to an ongoing Group Discussion I have titled, "Introduce Yourself to the Group!"

Creating an "Introduce Yourself to the Group!" post is a surefire way to (A) Make people feel welcome, (B) Get them excited about your Group and (C) Get them talking about their favorite topic – themselves!

These discussions will generate dozens of comments and likes, and people will immediately feel engaged and excited about what's going on inside your Group. Make sure that as the Group owner you go in and stoke the fire – respond to new comments by welcoming that person and saying something about him or her, and asking a follow up question to spur another comment. Or maybe let them know they should really connect with Jane Smith in the Group since both of them cater to a particular audience, etc.

Think of yourself like the host of the world's biggest virtual cocktail party. You want to make people feel welcome, and you want to bring value in whatever form you can – with connections and compliments, content you share, introductions to key people, links to resources, etc.

Along with that, make sure you're checking on your Group every single day to see what the latest activity is. Are there posts or comments awaiting moderation? Are there requests to join that you need to review and approve? Is there anybody new to the Group that you're not directly connected to that you need to send an invite to?

That last point is important. Think about it – someone you don't know and aren't connected to requested to join *your* Group. Just that act alone means they obviously find you and the value you're bringing useful. Why wouldn't you want to directly connect and get to know the person better?

Just have a simple copy-and-paste invitation ready to go that says, "Jane, thanks so much for joining my group on Debt Collection Marketing Tips, excited to have your insight and input added to the mix! I'd love to connect directly as well and learn more about your what you're up to!"

Make sure you are a 1st level connection with *everyone* in your Group. Also, do your best to spur more conversation whenever you see a comment or a new discussion posted. Ask open-ended questions, or ask people specifically, by name, what they think about issue XYZ. The more active your Group, the more people outside the Group will see and hear about it, and eventually join as a result.

SWAM = Site Wide Auto Moderation

Yet another reason to work like a psycho to build your personal LinkedIn Group is the dreaded advent of SWAM, or Site Wide Auto Moderation. It basically means that when you try to post your content inside of other LinkedIn Groups, if even *one* moderator in one of those Groups doesn't like your post, he or she can flag you as a spammer, and then your entire account *automatically* gets SWAM'd, meaning NONE of your posts or comments will show up in ANY of your Groups until someone approves them.

LinkedIn introduced SWAM in an effort to cut down on all the sales pitches and self-promotion that have plagued its Groups from Day One, but oftentimes you can get unfairly punished because one cranky moderator decided your post was too promotional.

What SWAM does is immediately cut your legs out from under you in every single LinkedIn Group you're a part of. All of a sudden, nobody will see your posts or comments until someone moderates and approves them.

All the more reason to focus on building YOUR Group. Not only is it your personal fishing pond that you're stocking with your ideal prospects, but it's also the one place where you can post anything you want without being SWAM'd!

One last tip: You can change the name of your LinkedIn Group. So if the one you started with doesn't seem to be working, or if you made the mistake of naming the Group after your company but don't want to start over, you can go under "Manage" and change the Group name. However, LinkedIn only lets you do this a few times, so choose wisely.

Other Groups – What to do

As I mentioned earlier in the book, you *do* want to join as many LinkedIn Groups (it will allow you to be in a maximum of 50) in your industry or niche as possible.

Not only are these Groups great for prospecting and finding your ideal customers, but they're also a great way to exponentially expand your reach to hundreds of thousands of additional prospects as well!

I'm going to start by showing you how to share to all LinkedIn groups at once. This is a *huge* tip. What you're going to do is go to your LinkedIn home page (just click "Home" on the menu). Once you're there, you'll see a little box where you can post an update or share some content.

IMPORTANT: This little trick *only* works when you're sharing an update that includes a link to a website or blog post. If you just do a text update or upload a photo, this trick will NOT work!

So here's the deal. You've written a great blog post or have a news story from a website that you know your audience would be interested in.

What you do is *first* share this content (your text plus the website link) as an individual LinkedIn status update. That will result in a new update to your news feed that includes whatever text you've inserted along with a box that pulls up the website or blog post you linked to.

Once this new post shows up in your news feed, hit "Share" underneath your post.

Delete

John Nemo

If your a debt collection agency in today's media environment, the bottom line is this: You need to tell your story. Because if you don't, nobody else will. And when your agency does speak, you need to use REAL people. I cannot emphasize that enough!

The One Simple Secret to Better PR for Collection Agencies

Insidearm.com · I cannot count how many times I've taken a reporter inside a debt collection agency and introduced him or her to the collections staff, then watched as the reporter came away amazed that debt collectors are regular, everyday people.

Like · Comment · Share · 1 second ago

LinkedIn will pull up a new box that allows you to re-share the post you just made. You can post it as a status update (which you just did, duh, so uncheck this box!), or you can Post to Groups (bingo!) or you can send to individual connections.

For this exercise, I want you to click "Post to Groups." Once you do that, LinkedIn expands the box and allows you to type in the name of *every single Group* you're a member of. Just start with the letter "A" and go through the whole alphabet. As soon as you type just one letter, LinkedIn will pull up a list of all the Groups you're a member of that start with that letter.

Click on the Group you want your post to be submitted to, and then do it again with the next one. Again! And again! (I feel like Herb Brooks in the movie *Miracle* when he's making the 1980s U.S. Olympic hockey team skate over and over in a conditioning drill – "Again! Again! Again!") This is an easy and instant way to share your content with up to 50 Groups (and potentially hundreds of thousands of your ideal prospects) all at once!

The key with this trick is to come up with an irresistible title for your Group discussion. Copyblogger.com's Free eBook on writing magnetic headlines is a great resource, so I'd suggest you grab it right away. Another method that works well on LinkedIn Groups is using an open-ended question as the title of your Group post. The reason being, a question automatically prompts people to formulate an answer in their heads and feel compelled to respond.

You really, really, REALLY need to come up with creative and curiosity-inducing headlines for your posts on LinkedIn. I can't tell you how much great content has never been read online because somebody put a crappy headline on top of it!

Think about the hyper fast, ultra-distracted environment we live in today. People on LinkedIn Groups are going to be quickly scrolling or flipping through posts or headlines as fast as they can to see if something catches their attention. And no matter how valuable, insightful or awesome the content you're sharing might be, if nobody stops to read it, what's the point?

Listen, it's hard. Copywriting and headline writing takes practice and study to perfect. Resources like Copyblogger.com will help you, and there are plenty of copy and paste templates you can try as well.

The biggest thing to remember is this: *Does your headline invoke some sort of curiosity or emotion as a result of reading it?* If it does, your chances of people clicking on your headline go *way* up.

LinkedIn Groups = Dysfunction Junction

There is a major shakeup going on right now inside of LinkedIn Groups. Many moderators are requiring that you do *not* share links to outside blog posts or websites in your submissions. In fact, some moderators will automatically delete posts that have links in them.

The reasoning is sound enough: They want to keep your post and the resulting discussion "on" LinkedIn instead of just having everyone jump off and go over to your website to read what you're talking about. These moderators view their LinkedIn Groups as a place to exchange ideas, talk shop and help each other, and that this happens best *within* the Group comments area. Also, too many people just throw up a quick post with a link to a sales page and no real content in the actual Group discussion area, and get SWAM'd (remember that?), blocked or deleted as a result.

Yet, as I just explained to you, LinkedIn *only* makes it possible to post to all your Groups at once if you have a link to an outside website or blog post in your status update!

(Shakes fist at LinkedIn for second time!)

With that in mind, you have to experiment a bit and hedge your bets too.

For starters, you'll want to periodically check whether or not your posts and submissions are showing up in a certain Group you're a member of. Just go to the Group you want to check on, and click "Your Activity" under your photo. It will take you a page where you can see what's happened to the submissions and comments you've made. Are they showing up on the Group's "Discussion" tab? Are they stuck in moderation purgatory? Have they all been moved to the dreaded "Promotions" tab? (To check this, click on the "Promotions" tab and then click on "Promotions you've started" to see if all your posts are ending up in there.) Have they just disappeared, meaning the moderator has deleted them without telling you why?

You'll want to see which Groups are giving you love (posting your content in the "Discussion" area without much delay or drama) and which are being dinks (not posting your content at all, holding it in moderation forever, shoving it into the "Promotions" tab, etc.)

(Yes, I just used the word "dink" in a book about LinkedIn. It was a huge diss in the 1980s, trust me! The next person you see, say this: "This Nemo guy is such a dink." Judging by their response, they'll either be 1980s savvy or have no clue what you're talking about.)

Inside of Groups, you do have the option to privately message Group Owners or Managers, and it's always a good idea to try and send them a polite message like this:

"Hi [NAME]. Just noticed my posts aren't showing up in the Discussion area. Is there something I'm doing wrong? I noticed many of my posts and comments are either being held in moderation, moved to Promotions or outright deleted. I LOVE being a part of this Group and really do want to add value and insight that helps everyone, so please let me know if I can do anything different to ensure my content gets shared in the Discussion area. Thanks!"

You also might quickly fall victim to SWAM (Site Wide Auto Moderation), and that will be another reason none of your posts or comments show up right away when you leverage the "post to all your Groups at once" trick that I just taught you.

Again, if this happens, you can individually go into each Group and ask the Manager/Moderator to remove the "Requires Moderation" listing on your account, but it's a pain and time consuming for both you *and* the moderators to do this.

This all points back to what I said earlier – focus *most* on YOUR LinkedIn Group and growing it as big as possible.

Consider the other LinkedIn Groups you're in valuable for two reasons – (1) Mining for prospects and (2) A place where you can oftentimes get your content pushed out in front of a much larger audience than you have inside your own Group.

One more quick tip: LinkedIn Groups are a great place to take the temperature of your prospects. What types of questions are they posting? What are they complaining about? What are they wishing there was a solution for? When you see posts like that, you should do two things. First, create a public comment to the person that offers your advice on how to solve the issue. Second, click "Reply Privately" under the person's name and copy and paste that same text into a LinkedIn Message. It will go straight to their inbox on LinkedIn, and that way you're assured they'll see what you had to say. The public comment is also good, because (assuming it's approved and posted) it shares your wisdom and insight with the entire "peanut gallery" of people online who have dropped in on this discussion or shared similar thoughts.

See how this works? You build your credibility and authority quickly when you come in and solve problems for people without asking for anything in return.

One other way to "experiment" with your posts to LinkedIn Groups is to put more text into the actual "Group Discussion" part of your post. Rather than just saying, "Check out our new blog post on 3 tips to improve your online sales conversions!", instead put some text into the Group Discussion section (right under your title) that says something like, "Curious – what are other small business owners seeing out there in terms of best online sales practices right now? What's working really well for you to convert and close sales online? Would love to hear any advice/insight others want to share. In that spirit, I put together a post over on our blog about the top 3 tips I'm seeing work for our business. I'll highlight them briefly below, and of course you can always jump over to our blog too. [Insert some tips and highlights from the blog post.] What do you think? Would love to hear what's working for you these days!"

This gives lazy people who don't want to leave LinkedIn and go over to your blog a way to get the "meat" of what you're saying right in front of them, and then instantly react/engage with you around it. Plus, you still have a link to your blog for those that want to jump over and see the full post, and in the process they're also exposed to all the other lead capturing tools and bells and whistles that your website offers.

CHAPTER 5

Proven:

How to **create content** on LinkedIn that establishes **your credibility** and **attracts** your **ideal customers**!

Imagine for a moment that you're a famous movie star like Brad Pitt. When you walk into a bar, all the beautiful people rush forward, fawning over you, thrusting slips of paper into your hand with their phone numbers and buying you drinks.

You're the person everybody wants to be with. You're the person everybody wants to talk to. You're the person everybody wants to work with.

OK, confession time: I can't make that happen for you in real life. But I *can* show you a technique to make it happen on LinkedIn!

Seriously: How great would it be to have people on LinkedIn literally putting their phone number in the public comments and singing "Call me, maybe!" every time you posted inside a Group?

Trust me, it's way easier to make this a reality than it is to hang at the bar with the likes of Brad Pitt.

The Key to LinkedIn Love

The secret is what I call "reverse-engineering" the product or service you want to sell by turning it into the perfect LinkedIn Group post. If you're able to do that, AND share it with the right audience, you're going to start feeling like the Brad Pitt of LinkedIn Groups! (Notice I didn't say "look like the Brad Pitt" – we can only work with what we've got, right?)

One LinkedIn Group Post = $7,000

Here's the story of how one short post inside a LinkedIn Group got me three sales leads and resulted in a $7,000 marketing project.

I was trying to figure out a way to sell more of my video marketing services to clients. I *love* making videos and being creative, and I also have seen firsthand the massive value video can bring to a brand, business or individual.

At the time, I was staying faithful to my niche approach and really only marketing to debt collection agency owners. So I went into a LinkedIn Group where my ideal prospects (debt collection agency executives) were hanging out. But instead of just *asking* for a sale or *claiming* authority, I *demonstrated* it.

I created a post titled, "3 Reasons Video Marketing is Critical for Your Collection Agency!" and then I put in some text

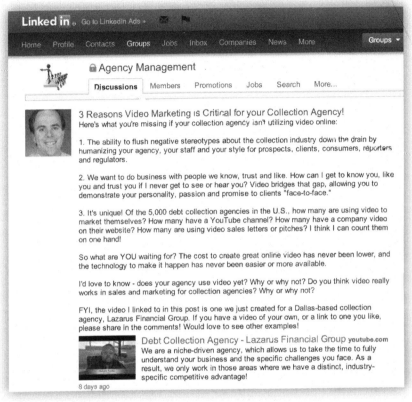

explaining each of the reasons in more detail. I made it *specific* to their industry and talked about how video could solve some of their key challenges – bad reputation in the media, lack of people finding their agency in Google Searches, failure to "humanize" their agency and people for new clients, etc. I added incentive and urgency by explaining that I wasn't seeing *anybody* in the debt collection industry using video like this, so the early adopters were going to get the biggest "wow" factor for rushing in and doing it first.

I closed with a call to action: "Hey, if your debt collection agency has done video marketing, how has it gone? Share a link to your marketing video here in the comments so we can all see it and get ideas. I'll get things started by sharing a video our agency recently did for a client."

I then pasted in a YouTube link to a client video we'd done.

Within a day I had two people put their phone number in the *public comments* asking me to call them with a bid on how much I'd charge to do a similar video for their agency. I had others put in the public comments or direct messages to me that they too wanted more info on my video marketing services!

Michael Levitzke • Hi John,

My name is Mike Levitzke. Owner of Hudson Acceptance, LLC. I would love to touch base with you and discuss services you can provide my company. I will be in office all next week. ▮▮▮▮▮▮▮▮▮▮▮

Regards
Mike

1 day ago • Unlike   👍 1

See how amazing that is?

It's all about reverse-engineering the product or service you want to sell and putting out content that draws people in, helps them see the immediate *value* and *benefit* of what you're talking about, and then leaves them with a subtle hint about that fact that YOU can provide this service or product for them right now!

That type of post does two very important things. First, it places YOU as an expert when it comes to, say, video marketing, and as someone people will want to follow and pay attention to as a trusted resource on all things video. Second, there will be some who read the post and decide, "This guy really makes a good point and knows his stuff. Plus, I loved his sample video from the comments. I'm going to find out how much he'd charge us for a video like that!"

Another option in this scenario might be to start your post with an open-ended question: "Does your Debt Collection Agency use video in its marketing efforts? Why or why not?" Your post can still share the value/benefit mentioned above, but your title might work better in triggering people to respond and engage since you're asking a direct question.

A third option is simply to monitor the Groups you're in for opportunities to share your wisdom in the comments. This is a great way to find people who are looking for what you have to offer, and immediately impressing them by adding your insight by answering their questions in the comment area.

Big Tip – Scripts + Notes!

I've got several scripts and notes saved on my computer for every different type of LinkedIn interaction I have with people. Whether it's an invite (from within a Group, from inside *my* Group, from a random stranger who looked at my profile page, etc.) I create and save a basic "script" to work from. I also save every single long answer or comment I create on LinkedIn Groups as a note. That way, when the same question inevitably comes up again inside a Group, or comes in as a 1-on-1 LinkedIn message, I can just copy, paste and clean up my response in a few seconds rather than writing the whole thing out again.

People freak out, because they think you literally sat down and wrote out that 600-word answer *just for them!* And in a way, you did.

Bottom line: I can't tell you how many hours that's saved me, and how it's enabled me to accomplish so much more as a result. Make sure you establish a way to save and organize your most used invite texts, LinkedIn posts, answers and comments.

Big News = We're all "LinkedIn Influencers" Now!

I recently nerded out on Netflix and watched an entire documentary on LinkedIn. The most interesting thing one of the head honchos at LinkedIn said was this: *"We want LinkedIn to be the place where people are creating and delivering the content you want to do your job today."*

Did you catch that line about "creating content?"

As of this writing, LinkedIn was unrolling a *huge* new endeavor based on their popular LinkedIn Influencer program. If you're not familiar with it, the "Influencer" program features big names like Martha Stewart, Richard Branson and Suze Orman basically *blogging right on LinkedIn* with their thoughts and tips on strategic partnerships, employee management, entrepreneurship and other work-related topics.

Anyway, at some point in the very near future (if not already!) *all of us* are going to have this ability to create and share new blog posts and other types of content right on LinkedIn.

If you're working for LinkedIn, it's a brilliant move. Having us all create and share our content right on LinkedIn's built-in blogging platform means we're all going to be spending *way* more time on the site both creating and consuming content. And more time on the site means LinkedIn gets to charge advertisers even more for those display ads and sponsored updates that we're seeing pop up all over the place.

"Starting today, LinkedIn is opening up our publishing platform to our members, giving them a powerful new way to build their professional brand," LinkedIn announced on its official blog. "When a member publishes a post on LinkedIn, their original content becomes part of their professional profile, is shared with their trusted network and has the ability to reach the largest group of professionals ever assembled. Now members have the ability to follow other members that are not in their network and build their own group of followers. Members can…[post] photos, images, videos and their original presentations on SlideShare."

If you want to read more about the possibilities this presents, Duct Tape Marketing's John Jantsch published an informative post about his first impressions of LinkedIn's new content publishing platform.

With nearly 300 million users worldwide and growing at a clip of 2 new members every second, LinkedIn is obviously betting big on content marketing becoming an even more integral part of its user experience. By essentially giving all of us our own on-site blogging platform, the sky's now the limit in terms of creating ready-made, platform-friendly content that can spread rapidly across the world's largest social media network for professionals.

It's also going to create a ton of spam and annoying sales pitches, but that's unavoidable at this point.

With of all that in mind, here are three ways I see you being able to create contagious content that will appeal to your target audience on LinkedIn:

1. Image + Text.

Following in the footsteps of Instagram, Pinterest and other popular visual sharing platforms, LinkedIn has made it easy for users to directly upload images to individual status updates, company pages, profiles and more.

In fact, some of the most popular posts on LinkedIn involve visuals mixed with some type of text.

John Nemo

Can I get an "Amen" here?

If Your Profile Does This...

LinkedIn member
This member chose to be
shown as anonymous

LinkedIn member
This member chose to be
shown as anonymous

Prospects Do This...

Like (18) · Comment (10) · Share · 13d ago

Jon Stillwell likes:

  Silvia Lazarte

Like (109,856) · Comment (4,432) · Share · 1h ago

You'll notice, alas, that silly cat photos have indeed made their way onto LinkedIn, along with "Are you a Genius" quizzes

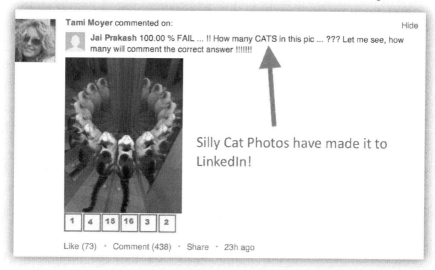

Silly Cat Photos have made it to LinkedIn!

and other types of visual content that one wouldn't typically associate with a "professional" network.

However, there *can* be a time for you to share "fun" content like this as a change of pace to your more career or work-focused content offerings. When done right, it will build engagement and grow your audience as a result.

Not a Graphic Designer? No Worries!

Creating an image + text piece of content is easier than you think. If you have a desktop application like PowerPoint, it's quite easy to import an image, overlay some text and then export the slide as a JPG file. You can also find a bevy of free online tools like Pinwords as well.

Even better, you can use free iPhone Apps like WordSwag to instantly create and share text + image creations right from your mobile phone. WordSwag makes it extra easy, offering you dozens of stock photos and cool fonts to choose from so you can quickly create an image + text offering in just a few seconds.

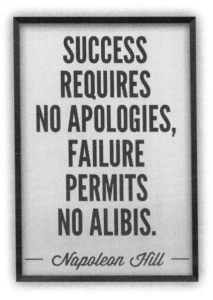

One important reminder when posting visual content – ask your audience to *do* something with it! Make a clear call to action such as "Give this a Like or Share if you agree!" so viewers help spread your content around LinkedIn.

2. SlideShare Presentations

Much has been written about SlideShare and its value for both SEO and visual appeal, so I won't belabor the point here. If you're not familiar with it, SlideShare is a website that allows you to upload PowerPoint presentations and other types of documents and then embed them on websites, blogs, etc. People can download them, flip through them online and leave comments and "likes" as well.

Because LinkedIn *owns* SlideShare, it goes the extra mile to make sure your SlideShare presentations display well on both its desktop *and* mobile platforms, which is always a bonus considering how many people are accessing LinkedIn through its mobile apps.

Slideshare is also a nice content marketing play because its premium accounts (which cost around $19 per month) allow you to add video inside a slide presentation and embed lead capture buttons as well.

Also, if you're already creating a PowerPoint for an in-person presentation or webinar, it's a no-brainer to upload and share it via SlideShare as well.

3. Videos

Short of meeting someone face-to-face, there's nothing better than video when it comes to doing business online. When done well, video humanizes you and your brand/company, triggers powerful emotions and engagement with your viewers and builds the type of trust and likability that are critical to moving someone from stranger to paying customer. It's also fantastic for SEO – remember, Google owns YouTube and now integrates those videos into search results.

If you're not comfortable being on camera, you can still create powerful videos that get shared widely. Consider using screen recording software such as EasyVideoSuite or Camtasia to create "How to" videos that walk viewers through a series of useful tips or strategies on a certain topic. If you go that route, it's worth investing in a USB microphone that plugs into your laptop to make sure your audio is high quality. (There are a ton of options out there, but one of the better high-end mics I've found is the Blue Yeti.)

Lastly, a great trick I love to use involves mixing in stock video footage. One of the best sites out there to find free or next-to-free stock video is VideoBlocks. (You'll also find tons of great stock video on sites like Shutterstock too, but it costs substantially more.)

The reason stock video matters is that it can help illustrate a point visually, thereby breaking up the monotony of you talking into the camera or showing us your computer screen nonstop.

Once you create and upload your videos to YouTube, you can also use an online service like SpeechPad to have a transcription made. Then, when you share your video on LinkedIn, you can include some text as well from the transcription to make the post even more valuable to your audience.

Final Thoughts on Content

Creating high-quality, contagious content is critical when it comes to being successful with social media. And with LinkedIn making such a big splash on the content creation side of things, it's going to be more important than ever to have something valuable to say – and share – in that space as well. Play to your strengths, be creative and don't be afraid to be human. Just because LinkedIn is a "professional" network doesn't mean you can't slip in a fun photo or showcase your personality from time to time with your content!

CHAPTER 6

Prophesy
Where is **LinkedIn Headed**?

One of the main reasons I waited so long to write this book was that I was worried that by the time I published it, the technology and user interface on LinkedIn would change so much that it would make my content and screen shots look outdated.

Well, those technology tweaks might still happen, but as you've noticed with this book, I've focused *way* more on the strategy (or, as George W. Bush likes to say, "stra-te-gery") behind leveraging LinkedIn for lead generation and new customers.

I *do* think LinkedIn is going to keep growing like crazy. As I mentioned earlier in the book, it's adding two new members every second or about 63 million members a year. I think the "global" element of LinkedIn is also going to be huge in the coming months, with more and more of us connecting and engaging with people from all over the planet.

In fact, it seems like I get multiple requests each day to connect with people from Europe, Asia, Africa…and most are relevant to what I do and the industries I serve. So I think we'll see more and more of that as the world continues to shrink due to social media and how hyper-connected we all are now.

Another area where I've really seen LinkedIn responding well is with their line of mobile apps – LinkedIn, Pulse and CardMunch, to name a few. LinkedIn realizes more and more of us are consuming content and doing our social networking on mobile devices, and I'm glad to see the company beefing up its mobile apps so often.

As far as *how* LinkedIn is going to be used, I think we'll see a massive spike in the amount of native content being created and shared right on LinkedIn with its new blogging platform.

I haven't mentioned LinkedIn Company Pages in this book, but they definitely do have value for large companies that can't easily have one person be the "face" of the business and do the 1-on-1, humanized marketing that works so well for smaller businesses and consultants/coaches like me.

LinkedIn Company Pages are also useful in terms of SEO value, plus I like the idea of using "Sponsored Updates" via your Company Page to reach fans that aren't yet "following" your company but might be interested in what you have to say or the value you provide. It seems like the brightest "paid" option I see on LinkedIn right now if you have ad dollars you want to spend.

Speaking of LinkedIn Advertising, I think it is, as of this writing, pretty much a first class disaster. The display ads program is clunky, *way* overpriced (unless you like paying $4.00 to $6.00 per click!) and difficult to use. Plus the results are pretty minimal based on everyone I've talked to and my own forays into using it.

I suspect LinkedIn will do better with "sponsored updates" and will likely start giving us an option to "boost" our new blog posts that we create on LinkedIn like you can do with Facebook in order to reach a bigger or more targeted audience.

Honestly, when looking at the "future" of LinkedIn and how we should all be leveraging it, I think we all need to hop in a DeLorean (yes, another 1980s reference!) like Marty and Doc in *Back to the Future* and return to 1936. That's when Dale Carnegie published *How to Win Friends and Influence People,* which remains a timeless field guide on how to build influence and make money no matter what niche you're in.

As long as you keep your approach on LinkedIn client facing, as long as you always convey an immediate benefit + value to the people you interact with, and as long as you stay away from self-serving sales pitches like the plague, you'll be in good shape.

That, and eat plenty of Super Pretzels!

Bonuses + Resources

have lots of free videos, trainings and other resources I want to share with you. If you haven't already, check out www. LinkedInRiches.com and you'll discover scores of posts and videos that compliment and in some cases even expand upon what I've shared here in the book. Also make sure to sign up for my email list so I can keep you looped in on more new trainings and the like!

Special Offer – LinkedIn Riches Premium Training

I also want to make you a *very* special offer. If you've enjoyed the book, taken furious notes and all the while wished there was a corresponding series of online, "how to" videos teaching you everything you need to do, step-by-step, I have your answer – *LinkedIn Riches Video Training!*

LinkedIn Riches Video Training is a series of video modules hosted online that walk you through *exactly* how to implement everything I've been teaching you in this book.

In the videos, I help illustrate for you the *exact* method I used to do more than $135,000 in revenue in just 90 days using LinkedIn. The simple formula I teach you in these videos works in any niche, takes just a few minutes a day to apply and will drive targeted, ready-to-buy prospects to your virtual front door. It doesn't matter what your experience level is when it comes to LinkedIn – literally anyone can do this!

Each video module includes transcripts so you don't have to worry about taking notes while you watch. The modules are set up so that you can easily pause the video, open up a new window or tab on your browser, apply what you just learned to your own LinkedIn profile or Group page, and then go back

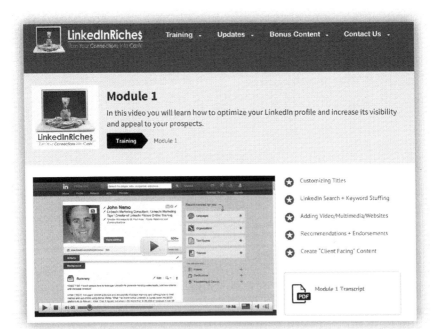

to the training and resume the video. LinkedIn Riches is the perfect "hands on" companion to this book because the videos *show* you in a can't-fail way how to take action on what you've learned here!

One other special treat if you decide to purchase the LinkedIn Riches online training: Bonus Modules!

I went out and interviewed a virtual "Who's-Who" of the Marketing, PR, SEO and Journalism professionals via Google+ Hangouts. I then transformed those 1-on-1 interviews into practical training sessions you can access, including:

- How to get Ranked #1 on Google Search: 1-on-1 Interview/Advice From SEO Expert Lee Odden.

- "Newsjacking" Interview With Bestselling Marketing Author David Meerman Scott.

- Crisis PR Tips/Coaching From Industry Insider Jon Austin.

- Content Marketing – How to Instantly Attract Targeted Prospects Online with your Content.

- Video Tips/Secrets From Longtime TV and Radio Producers – How to Get Yourself On-Air and In-Demand for live TV and radio interviews!

These bonus videos are all included for FREE if you grab *LinkedIn Riches Video Training* via the link below.

LinkedInRiche$.com
Turn Your **Connections** *Into* **Cash!**

YES! I Want to Leverage LinkedIn for Nonstop Sales Leads!

Discover the *exact* method I used to do more than $135,000 in revenue in just 90 days using LinkedIn! In less than 60 minutes, you'll unlock the secrets to making money on the world's largest business networking platform. The simple formula I teach you works in *any* niche, takes just a few minutes a day to apply and will drive targeted, ready-to-buy prospects to your virtual front door! It doesn't matter what your experience level is when it comes to LinkedIn – literally *anyone* can do this! Find out RIGHT NOW just how easy it is!

Here's the link: www.LinkedInRiches.com/BookOffer

When you purchase LinkedIn Riches Video Training, you get *instant* access to everything, including all the bonus modules. I'll also throw in a 30-Day Money Back Guarantee – if you're not happy with what you find inside LinkedIn Riches, just email me within 30 days of your purchase and I'll refund your money – no questions asked.

(Somewhere I can hear a used car salesman yelling, "It's the biggest no-brainer in the history of no-brainers!")

Public Speaking + Presenting

I also love public speaking and on-site presentations and training, so if you're interested in bringing me in to talk with your trade association, company or group, shoot me an email at JohnNemoPR@gmail.com.

More About the Author

John Nemo is a former Associated Press Reporter, Award-Winning PR Director and Social Media Consultant who generated more than $135,000 in revenue for his business in just 90 days using LinkedIn.

He is the creator of www.LinkedInRiches.com, an online training course that helps brands, businesses and individuals leverage LinkedIn to generate more sales leads, add clients and increase revenue.

A sought after public speaker and presenter, Nemo also offers 1-on-1 coaching and consulting services for clients across the world. In addition, he is the CEO and Founder of Nemo Media Group, a Minneapolis-based marketing agency that provides graphic and website design, content creation, video marketing and PR services to clients across the U.S.

The author of five previous books, John Nemo has written for nearly 150 different national and regional publications over the past 20 years, including *Sports Illustrated* online, *The Philadelphia Inquirer*, *The Chicago Sun-Times*, *The Arizona Republic* and *The Minneapolis Star Tribune*.

As a PR Director, his 2010 publicity campaign for the Minnesota Nurses Association (MNA) reached an estimated 133 million people in 120 days and would have cost $5 million in advertising costs to duplicate. Nemo's 2010 Social Media campaign for the Minnesota Nurses Association led to 496,000 Facebook page views in 90 days, along with 342,000 blog views, 97,000 YouTube views and 2,850 comments.

Prior to his time at MNA, John Nemo worked as the PR Director for ACA International, The Association of Credit and Collection Professionals, as an on-air talent and producer for KTIS-AM radio, and as a reporter for the *Associated Press* and *The Arizona Republic*.

John Nemo lives near St. Paul, Minnesota with his wife, Sara, their three sons and Rosie the dog. Learn more about him online at www.LinkedInRiches.com or www.NemoMediaGroup.com. Reach him via email at JohnNemoPR@gmail.com and connect on LinkedIn at http://www.linkedin.com/in/hirejohnnemo.

Made in the USA
Lexington, KY
10 July 2014